University of Toronto Installation Lectures / *1958*

1958 University of Toronto Installation Lecture

3 LECTURES

Frye / Kluckhohn / Wigglesworth

INTRODUCTION

Murray G. Ross, M.A., Ed.D., Vice-President, University of Toronto

THE HUMANITIES

Northrop Frye, M.A., LL.D., D.D., F.R.S.C., Chairman of the
Department of English, Victoria College

THE SOCIAL SCIENCES

Clyde Kluckhohn, M.A., Ph.D., L.H.D., Professor of Anthropology,
Harvard University

THE PRACTICAL SCIENCES

V. B. Wigglesworth, C.B.E., M.D., F.R.S., Quick Professor of Biology,
University of Cambridge

INTRODUCTION

by Murray G. Ross, Vice-President, University of Toronto

The three papers that follow comprise the Installation Lectures which were presented as part of the ceremonies associated with the installation of Claude T. Bissell as eighth President of the University of Toronto on November 22nd, 1958.

The Committee planning the Installation events had in mind that the occasion should be used to illustrate and reinforce the ends to which a great University is dedicated. Whatever else a University may be, it must be a place where ideas are projected, criticized, and evaluated. Hence a group of lectures by scholars, with manifest excellence in such treatment of ideas, was decided upon. The fields of Humanities, the Social Sciences, and the Natural Sciences were selected because of their traditional and central importance in the University. We were fortunate in being able to secure Professor Northrop Frye of Victoria College, University of Toronto, Professor Clyde Kluckhohn of Harvard University, and Professor V. B. Wigglesworth of Cambridge University for these lectures, thus assuring the fulfilment of the purposes the Committee had in mind. In part by design and in part by accident, the three lecturers chosen linked Canada with the United States and Great Britain, and the University of Toronto with Harvard University and Cambridge University. We hope this is a happy omen of the future.

It might be of interest to note that these three lectures were given simultaneously in the three largest lecture halls available on the campus. While over 1,600 students and members of staff crowded into the halls to hear the lectures, at least 1,200 persons were turned away because of lack of accommodation. We hope the wide interest in these lectures is evidence of the continuing commitment of this University community to scholarship and to scholarly pursuits.

HUMANITIES IN A NEW WORLD

by Northrop Frye, Chairman of the Department of English, Victoria College

The installing of a young president is a natural time for a university to take stock of itself and speculate about its immediate future. It is quite possible, of course, that it has no future apart from the approaching extermination of the human race. But there is clearly no point in my going on to a third sentence unless I can assume at least a chance that this nightmare, like other nightmares, may come to overreach itself through the very intensity of its horror. If there is that chance, the immediate future seems inviting enough, and not only by contrast. Apart from personal knowledge, one feels reassured both by what President Bissell is and what he is not. What he is not is a high priest of some mystical administrative elite: what he is is a professor of English.

His early studies were on Samuel Butler, and so he must have absorbed, at an impressionable age, some of the things that that sharp-tongued writer said about universities in his day. In his satirical romance *Erewhon*, published in 1872, Butler describes the "Colleges of Unreason," which taught mainly the "hypothetical languages," languages of great difficulty that never existed. The professors were obsessed with the notion that in this world all well-bred people must compromise, hence they instructed their students never to commit themselves on any point. They had professorships of Inconsistency and Evasion, and students were plucked in examinations for a lack of vagueness in their answers. There was however a more modern feeling that examinations should be abolished altogether, the competition involved being regarded as "self-seeking and unneighborly." The strictest of the professors was the professor of Worldly Wisdom, who was also President of the Society for the Suppression of Useless Knowledge, and for the Completer Obliteration of the Past. Butler concludes that at these Colleges "The art of sitting gracefully on a fence has never, I should think, been brought to greater perfection."

The point of Butler's satire is that the more the university tries to remain aloof from society, the more slavishly it will follow the accepted patterns of that society. The tendencies that Butler ridicules are those of a social system in which the ideal is a gentlemanly amateur, with no definite occupation. The university that confronts President Bissell today still reflects accepted social attitudes, but those attitudes have changed, and the university has changed with them. The university is now well aware of its social function, and if it were not, public opinion would compel it to become so. Professors are still unwilling to commit themselves, but their reasons are no longer abstract social reasons, but concrete political ones.

Above all, the ideal of productivity, the vision of the unobstructed assembly line, has taken over the university as it has everything else. The professor today is less a learned man than a "productive scholar." He is trained in graduate school to become productive by an ingenious but simple device. It is a common academic failing to dream of writing the perfect book, and then, because no achievement can reach perfection, not writing it. One of the major scholarly enterprises on this campus, Professor Coburn's edition of the note-books of Coleridge, is the result of the fact that Coleridge never wrote his gigantic masterpiece, the treatise on the Logos that would tell the world what Coleridge knew, but hugged it to his bosom in the form of fifty-seven note-books. *Nous avons changé tout cela.* Our graduate student today must finish a thesis, a document which is, practically by definition, something that nobody particularly wants either to write or to read. This teaches him that it is more important to produce than to perfect, and that it is less anti-social to contribute to knowledge than to possess it.

In Butler's day there were no Ph.D's in English, but since then there has been a vast increase in the systematizing of scholarship. The modern library, with its stacks and microfilms; modern recordings, reproductions of pictures, aids in learning languages: all these are part of a technological revolution that has transformed the humanities equally with the sciences. There were Canadian poets and novelists a century ago, and critics who reviewed and discussed their work, but there was not the same sense of the systematic processing of literature that there is now, in the Canadian criticism in which President Bissell himself has taken a distinguished place. Of course, wherever there is a cult of productivity there is a good deal of hysteria. New students come along with reputations to make; new poets arise to be commented on; learned journals multiply and their subsidies divide; bibliographies lengthen, and so does the list of works that a scholar feels apologetic about not having read. There seems no answer to this steadily increasing strain on the scholarly economy except the Detroit answer, that next year's books will be still bigger, duller, fuller of superfluous detail, and more difficult to house. If I were speaking only to scholars in the humanities,

I should say merely that this is our business, and that we can take care of it. But as I am speaking to a wider public, I should like also to try to explain, if I can, what difference our business makes in the world.

I begin with the fact that the faculty of arts and sciences, or more briefly the faculty of arts, seems to be the centre of the University. A big modern university, like this one, could almost be defined as whatever group of professional schools in one town happens to be held together by a faculty of arts. We can have a university that is nothing but a faculty of arts; on the other hand, a professional school, set up by itself, is not a university, although it may resemble university life in many ways.

The reason for this is not hard to see as far as science is concerned. The university is the powerhouse of civilization, and the centre of the university has to correspond to the actual centres of human knowledge. Engineering is practical or applied science; medicine is really another form of applied science. And if we ask what it is that gets applied in these professions, the answer is clearly science, as conceived and studied in the faculty of arts. The basis of technology, or applied science, is a disinterested research, carried on without regard to its practical applications, ready to take the risk of being thought useless or socially indifferent or morally neutral, concerned only with developing the science, not with improving the lot of mankind. Technology by itself cannot produce the kind of scientist that it needs for its own development: at any rate, that seems to be the general opinion of those who are qualified to have an opinion on the subject.

Attached to the sciences are what we call the liberal arts or humanities. What are they doing at the centre of university life? Are they there because they must be there, or merely because they have always been there? Are they functional in the modern world, or only ornamental? The simplest way to answer these questions is to go back to the principle on which, in the Middle Ages, the seven liberal arts were divided into two groups. The two great instruments that man has devised for understanding and transforming the world are words and numbers. The humanities are primarily the *verbal* disciplines; the natural sciences are the numerical ones. The natural sciences are concerned very largely with measurement, and at their centre is mathematics, the disinterested study of numbers, or quantitative relationships. At the centre of the humanities, corresponding to mathematics, is language and literature, the disinterested study of words, a study which ranges from phonetics to poetry. Around it, corresponding to the natural sciences, are history and philosophy, which are concerned with the verbal organization of events and ideas.

And just as we have engineering and other forms of applied science, so there is a vast area of what we may call verbal technology, the use of words for practical or useful purposes. The two words practical and useful do not of course mean quite the same thing: some forms of verbal technology, like preaching, may be useful without always being practical; others, like advertising, may be practical without always being useful. Many of the university's professional schools— law, theology, education—are concerned with verbal technology, and so is every area of human knowledge that employs words as well as numbers, metaphors as well as equations, definition as well as measurement. A century ago the central subjects in arts were Classics and mathematics, Classics being restricted to Greek and Latin. Today the central subjects are still Classics and mathematics, but Classics has broadened out to take in all the languages in our cultural orbit, beginning with our own.

This seems clear enough: why are people so confused about the humanities, and more especially confused about literature? There are many answers, but the important one is quite simple. A student who learns only a few pages of Latin grammar will never see the point of having learned even that; and today he learns so little English in early life that the majority of our young people can hardly be said to possess even a native language. "I think," said Sir Philip Sidney, "(it) was a piece of the Tower of Babylon's curse, that a man should be put to school to learn his mother tongue." But it is no use pretending that the curse of Babel does not exist. Behind *Paradise Lost*, behind *Hamlet*, behind *The Faerie Queene*, lay years of daily practice in translating Latin into English, English into Latin, endless themes written and corrected and rewritten, endless copying and imitation of the Classical writers, endless working and reworking of long lists of rhetorical devices with immense Greek names. Discipline of this kind is apparently impossible in the modern school, where teachers are not only overworked but subjected to anti-literary pressures. They are encouraged, sometimes compelled, to substitute various kinds of slick verbal trash for literature; they are bedevilled with audiovisual and other aids to distraction; their curricula are prescribed by a civil service which in its turn responds to pressure from superstitious or prurient voters. In the verbal arts, the student of eighteen is about where he should be at fourteen, apart from what he does on his own with the help of a sympathetic teacher or librarian. To say this is not to reflect on the schools, but on the social conditions that cripple them.

So the student often enters college with the notion that reading and writing are elementary subjects that he mastered in childhood. He may never clearly have grasped the fact that there are differences in levels of reading and writing, as there are in mathematics between short division and integral calculus. He is disconcerted to find that, after thirteen years of schooling, he is still, by any civilized standard, illiterate. Further, that a lifetime of study will never bring him to the point at which he has read enough or can write well enough. Still, he is, let us say, an intelligent and interested student with a reasonable amount of good will—most students are, fortunately. He begins to try to write essays, perhaps without ever having written five hundred consecutive words in his life before, and the first results take the form of that verbal muddle which is best called jargon. He is now on the lowest rung of the literary ladder, on a level with the distributors of gobbledygook, double talk and officialese of all kinds; of propaganda, public relations and Timestyle; of the education textbook that is not lucky enough to be rewritten in the publisher's office.

By jargon I do not mean the use of technical terms in a technical subject. Technical language may make one's prose look bristly and forbidding, but if the subject is genuinely specialized there is no way to get out of using it. By jargon I mean writing in which words do not express meanings, but are merely thrown in the general direction of their meanings; writing which can always be cut down by two-thirds without loss of whatever sense it has. Jargon always unconsciously reveals a personal attitude. There is the blustering jargon that says to the reader, "Well, anyway, you know what I mean." Such writing exhibits a kind of squalid arrogance, roughly comparable to placing a spittoon on the opposite side of the room. There is the coy jargon which, like the man with one talent, wants to wrap up and hide away what it says so that no reader will be able to dig it. There is the dithering jargon that is afraid of the period, and jerks along in a series of dashes, a relay race whose torch has long since gone out. There is the morally debased jargon of an easily recognized type of propaganda, with its greasy clotted abstractions, its weaseling arguments, and its undertone of menace and abuse. There is the pretentious jargon of those who feel that anything readable must be unscientific. And finally, there is the jargon produced by our poor student, which is often the result simply of a desire to please. If he were studying journalism, he would imitate the jargon of journalism; as he is being asked to write by professors, he produces the kind of verbal cotton-wool which is his idea of the way professors write. What is worse, it is the way that a lot of them do write.

When teachers of the humanities attack and ridicule jargon, they do not do so merely because it offends their aesthetic sensibilities, offensive as it is in that respect. They attack it because they understand the importance of a professional use of words. The natural sciences, we said, are largely concerned with measurement, which means accurate measurement. In any subject that uses words, the words have to be used with precision, clarity and power, otherwise the statements made in them will be either meaningless or untrue. Lawyers, for example, use words in a way very different from the poets, but their use of them is precise in their field, as anyone who tries to draft a law without any legal training will soon discover. And what is true of law cannot be less true of sociology or metaphysics or literary criticism.

It is often thought that teachers of the humanities judge everything in words by a pedantic and rather frivolous standard of correctness. They don't care, it is felt, what one really means; all they care about is whether one says "between you and I," or uses "contact" and "proposition" as verbs. Now it is true that the humanities are based on the accepted forms of grammar, spelling, pronunciation, syntax and meaning. If a man says he will pay you what he owes you next Toisday, it is useful to know whether he means Tuesday or Thursday: if there were no accepted forms there could be no communication. Teachers in the humanities are also concerned with preventing words from being confused with other words, with preserving useful distinctions among words, with trying to make the methods of good writers in the past available for writers today, with trying to steer a civilized course between dictionary dictatorship and mob rule. Some snobbery is bound to be attached to the ability to use words correctly. We hear a good deal about that.

For some reason we hear less about the much greater amount of snob appeal in vulgarity. Most of the people who say "throwed" instead of "threw" know well enough that "threw" is the accepted form, but are not going to be caught talking good grammar. On other social levels there is a strong feeling that the natural destiny of those who can handle words properly is to form a kind of genteel servant class: ghost writers who turn out books and speeches for the unlettered great; secretaries who translate the gargles and splutters of their bosses into letters written in English; preachers and professors and speakers at clubs who function as middle-class entertainers. Such a conception of society is very like that of a P. G. Wodehouse novel, where the butler speaks in a formal nineteenth-century style and his wealthy young master talks like a mentally retarded child. Then again, as Henry James pointed out fifty years ago in his book *The American Scene*, there was a time when the absorption of the North American male in business led to the domination of all the rest of civilized life by the woman. The result has been that the word culture, which strictly means everything that man has accomplished since he came down out of the trees, has come to acquire a strongly feminine cast. This sense of the word survives in the silly clichés that people use to prevent themselves from thinking, such as "longhair," or, most fatuous and slovenly of them all, "ivory tower," a phrase which has become popular because it sounds vaguely female and sexual, like a calendar girl in *Esquire*. But this male absorption in business was the product of an expanding economy and weak labour unions: it is now drawing to a close, and in matters of culture the woman is being joined by what Henry James, with his usual delicacy, called her sleeping partner.

Our student, with a little practice, will soon advance from jargon to the beginnings of prose, which means advancing from an amateurish to a professional approach to words. To make such an advance involves an important moral and psychological change. Bad writers are like bad car-drivers: what they are doing is the unconscious expression of a way of life. The purveyors of jargon are like the man who honks and hustles his way through traffic to advertise the importance of his business, or the woman who wants to hit something in order to prove that she is helpless and appealing. The good car-driver regards his or her activity as a simple but highly specific skill, unconnected with the rest of the personality. The good writer is the writer who puts self-expression aside, and is ready to submit himself to the discipline of words.

In the past, and under the influence of the old faculty psychology, the different fields of study were correlated with different parts of the mind. Thus history was ascribed to the memory, poetry to the imagination, and philosophy and science to the reason. This way of thinking has left many traces in our day: it is still widely believed that a mathematician is an unemotional reasoner, and a poet a "genius," a word which usually means emotionally unbalanced. But, of course, any difficult study demands the whole mind, not pieces of it. Reason and a sense of fact are as important to the novelist as they are to the chemist; genius and creative imagination play the same role in mathematics they they do in poetry. A similar fallacy may be confusing our student at this critical point. I am, he perhaps feels, a conscious being; I know I can think; I know I have ideas that are waiting to be put into words. I wish somebody would show me how to express my ideas, instead of shoving all this poetry stuff at me. After all, poets put their *feelings* into words, so they can make sounds and pictures out of them; but that isn't what I want.

Every step in this chain of reasoning is wrong, so it is no wonder if the reasoner is confused. In the first place, thinking is not a natural process like eating or sleeping. The difficulty here is partly semantic: we are apt to speak of all our mental processes as forms of thought.

Musing, day-dreaming, associating, remembering, worrying: every slop and gurgle of our mental sewers we call thinking. If we are asked a question and can only guess at the answer, we begin with the words "I think." But real thinking is an acquired skill founded on practice and habit, like playing the piano, and how well we can think at any given time will depend on how much of it we have already done. Nor can we think at random: we can only add one more idea to the body of something we have already thought about. In fact we, as individuals or egos, can hardly be said to think at all: we link our minds to an objective body of thought, follow its facts and processes, and finally, if the links are strong enough, our minds become a place where something new in the body of thought comes to light.

It is the same with the imaginative thinking of literature. The great writer seldom regards himself as a personality with something to say: his mind to him is simply a place where something happens to words. T. S. Eliot compares the poet to a catalyzer, which accompanies but does not bring about the process it is used for; Keats speaks of the poet's negative capability; Wordsworth of his recollection in tranquility; Milton of the dictation of unpremeditated verse by a Muse. The place where the greatest fusions of words have occurred in English was in the mind of Shakespeare, and Shakespeare, as a personality, was so self-effacing that he has irritated some people into a frenzy of trying to prove that he never existed.

If the student were studying natural science, he would grasp this principle of objective thought very quickly. There can be no self-expressive approach to physics or chemistry: one has to learn the laws of the science first before one can have anything to express in it. But the same thing is true of the verbal disciplines. The student is not really struggling with his own ideas, but with the laws and principles of words. In any process of genuine thought that involves words, there can be no such thing as an inarticulate idea waiting to have words put around it. The words are the forms of which the ideas are the content, and until the words have been found, the idea does not exist.

A student of engineering may have extremely practical aims in entering that field, but he cannot get far without mathematics. Hence mathematics, though not in itself a practical subject, is practical enough for him. For a student who is going to engage in any verbal activity, the study of literature, not in itself a practical subject, is a practical necessity. The sciences deal with facts and truths, but mathematics sets one free from the particular case: it leads us from three apples to three, and from a square field to a square. Literature has the same function in the humanities. The historian is concerned with finding the right words for the facts; the philosopher, with finding the right words for the truth. As compared with the historian, the poet is concerned, Aristotle tells us, not with what happened but with the kind of thing that does happen. As compared with the philosopher, the poet is concerned, not with specific statements, but with the images, metaphors, symbols and verbal patterns out of which all directed thinking comes. Mathematics is useful, but pure mathematics, apart from its use, is one of the major disciplines of beauty. Poetry, is, in itself, beautiful, but if we think of it as merely decorative or emotional, that is because we have not learned to use it. We can build the most gigantic structures out of words and numbers, but we have constantly to return to literature and mathematics, because they show us the infinite possibilities that there are in words and numbers themselves. Sir James Jeans, speaking of the failure of nineteenth-century physics to build a mechanical model of the universe, says that the Supreme Architect of the universe must be a mathematician. A much older authority informs us that the Supreme Teacher of mankind was a story-teller, who never taught without a parable.

The humanities in the university are supposed to be concerned with criticism and scholarship, not with creation as such. At the centre of literature lie the "classics," the works that university teachers know they can respect, and the university student, *qua* student, is there to study them, not to write on his own. True, most writers of importance today are not only university graduates but university employees, at least in summer sessions. True, the untaught writer who sends a masterpiece to a publisher from out of nowhere is much more a figure of folklore than of actual literature. Still, the university does not try to foster the social conditions under which great literature can be produced. In the first place, we do not know what these conditions are; in the second place, we have no reason to suppose that they are good conditions. Just as doctors are busiest in an epidemic, so our dramatists and novelists may find their best subjects where decadence, brutality, or idiocy show human behaviour in its more fundamental patterns. Or the producer of literature himself may be a drunk, a homosexual, a Fascist, a philanderer; in short, he may want things that the university cannot guarantee to supply.

The university, therefore, addresses itself to the consumer of literature, not to the producer. The consumer of literature is the cultivated man, the man of liberal education and disciplined taste, for whose benefit the poet has worked, suffered, despaired, or even wrecked his life. What the university does try to do is to foster the social conditions under which literature can be appreciated. Many teachers of the humanities are anxious to stop at that point, especially those who wish

that they had been great poets instead. It is natural for them to insist
that critics and scholars have no real function except to brush off
the poet's hat and hand it to him. But a merely passive appreciation
of literature is not enough. As Gerard Manley Hopkins said:
"The effect of studying masterpieces is to make me admire and do
otherwise." He was a poet, but he has exactly defined, even for
non-poets, the effect of great writing, which is great because it is
infinitely suggestive, and encourages us not to imitate it,
but to do what we can in our own way. To appreciate literature is
also to use it, to absorb it into our own lives and activities. There
is unlikely to be much of a gap between what the humanities will do
in a new world and what they are trying to do in this one. Teachers
of the humanities understand the importance of what they are
doing, and in any new world worth living in, nine-tenths
of their effort would be to go on doing it. Still, I think they will
become increasingly interested in the ways in which words and
verbal patterns do affect human lives. They are likely to follow the
direction indicated by the poet Wallace Stevens in one of his
long discursive poems:

This endlessly elaborating poem
Displays the theory of poetry
As the life of poetry. A more severe,

More harassing master would extemporize
Subtler, more urgent proof that the theory
Of poetry is the theory of life.

A few years ago there was a great vogue for something called
"semantics," which purported to be, not simply a certain type of
literary study, but a panacea for human ills. People get neurotic, we
were told, by attaching private and emotional significances to words:
once they learn to use words properly, to bring them into alignment
with the world around them, their psychological distresses and
tensions will clear up. A minor advantage would be the abolishing
of literature, where words are so thickly coated with emotional
associations. Like other miraculous cures, semantics of this type
achieved a great success among the hysterical, but failed to do everything
it promised to do. It looks as though, as long as men are discussing
matters that affect their pocketbooks, their homes or their lives,
they will continue to attach emotional significance to the words
they use. Perhaps it would be better to recognize that there
is no short cut to verbal accuracy, and go back to study the poets,
who have not tried to get rid of emotion, but have tried to make
it precise. Nevertheless, the semanticists were right about the
importance of words in human life, about the immediacy and
intimacy of their impact, about their vast powers for good or for evil.

We use words in two ways: to make statements and arguments
and convey information, or what passes as such, and to appeal to the
imagination. The former is the province of history, philosophy and
the social sciences; the latter is the province of literature.
There is also a large intermediate area of what is called rhetoric,
the art of verbal persuasion, where both means are employed.
We are brought up to believe that words stand for things, and that
most of our experience with words takes the form of reported fact,
argument, and logical inference. This is a flattering self-delusion.
Most of our daily experience with words takes place on a low level
of the imagination—that is, it is sub-literary. I am writing this
on the subway, and my eye falls on an advertisement for heavy-duty
floor wax. Nothing could be more honestly factual; but even here
"heavy duty" is a metaphor, probably of military origin, and the
metaphor, with its imaginative overtones of ruggedness, strength and
endurance, is the focus of the sales appeal. If the advertiser
has something expensive or useless to sell, this sub-literary appeal is
stepped up. One cannot read far in advertising without encountering
over-writing, a too earnestly didactic tone, an uncritical acceptance
of snobbish standards, and obtrusive sexual symbolism. These are
precisely the qualities of inferior literature.

Then there are the other sub-literary areas of soap operas, movies,
magazine stories, jokes, comic strips, gossip. It is out of the steady
rain of imaginative impressions from these and similar quarters that
most people form their myths: that is, their notions of representative
human situations, of typical human characters and characteristics,
of what is inspiring and what is ridiculous, of the socially
acceptable and the socially outcast. It is here that the kind of
preferences develop which determine one to condemn or condone
segregation, to support or decry the United Nations, to vote for
Mr. Diefenbaker or for Mr. Pearson. For even election issues and
current events reach us chiefly through human-interest stories and
personal impressions. For better or worse, it is through his literary
imagination, such as it is, that modern man participates in society.

The responsible citizen, of course, tries to get away from mythical
stereotypes, to read better papers and seek out friends who have some
respect for facts and for rational discussion. But he will never
succeed in raising his standards unless he educates his imagination
too, for nothing can drive bad literature out of the mind except
good literature. In these days we have an exaggerated sense of the
power of argument and indoctrination. "Ideas are weapons" was
a once fashionable phrase, and during the war publishers carried
the slogan "books are weapons in the war of ideas." But arguments
and aggressive ideas have a very limited role to play in human life.

They that take the argument will perish by the argument; any statement that can be argued about at all can be refuted. The natural response to indoctrination is resistance, and nothing will make it successful except a well organized secret police. What can never be refuted is the underlying vision of life which all such arguments try to rationalize. The arguments are based on assumptions about what is worth living for or dying for; these are rooted in the imagination, and only the imagination can nourish them.

The distinction that we have made between the disciplines of words and numbers does not quite correspond to the distinction between the arts and the sciences. There are arts that do not depend on words, like music and painting, and there are sciences that do, like the social sciences. The real difference between art and science is expressed by Francis Bacon in *The Advancement of Learning*:

The use of (poetry) hath been to give some shadow of satisfaction to the mind of Man in those points where the Nature of things doth deny it, the world being in proportion inferior to the soul . . . And therefore (poetry) was ever thought to have some participation of divineness, because it doth raise and erect the Mind, by submitting the shews of things to the desires of the Mind, whereas reason doth buckle and bow the Mind unto the Nature of things.

The sciences, in other words, are primarily concerned with the world as it is: the arts are primarily concerned with the world that man wants to live in. The sciences have among other things the function of showing man how much he can realize of what he wants to do, and how much has to remain on the level of wish or fantasy. In between comes the area of applied science and applied art, where the process of realization is accomplished. Architecture is one obvious place in which science and art meet on a practical basis. Art, then, owes its existence to man's dissatisfaction with nature and his desire to transform the physical world into a human one. Religion itself, when it deals with ultimate things, uses the language of art, and speaks of an eternal city and a restored garden as the fulfilling of the soul's desires. The human imagination, which the arts address, is not an escape from reality, but a vision of the world in its human form.

Science continually evolves and improves: the scientist contributes to an expanding body of knowledge, and the freshman studying physics today can sit on the shoulders of Newton and Faraday, knowing things that they did not know. The arts, on the other hand, produce the classic or model, which may be equalled by something different, but is never improved on. The greatest artists have reached the limits of what their art can do: there is an infinite number

of limits to be reached, and artists of the future will reach many of
them, but it makes nonsense of the conception of art to think
of it as developing. The painters in the stone age caverns were as
highly developed as Picasso; Homer is as much a model for poets
today as he was for Virgil. We have as great art as humanity can
ever produce with us now. The natural direction of science, then,
is onward: it moves toward still greater achievements in the future.
The arts have this in common with religion, that their direction is not
onward into the future but upward from where we stand.

The point of contact between the arts and the human mind is the
moment of leisure, one of the most misunderstood words in the
language. Leisure is not idleness, which is neurotic, and still less
is it distraction, which is psychotic. Leisure begins in that moment
of consciousness peculiar to a rational being, when we become
aware of our own existence and can watch ourselves act, when we
have time to think of the worth and purpose of what we are doing,
to compare it with what we might or would rather be doing. It is
the moment of the birth of human freedom, when we are able to
subject what is actual to the standard of what is possible.
William Blake calls it the moment in the day that Satan cannot find.
It is a terrifying moment for many of us, like the opening of a
Last Judgement in the soul, and our highways and television sets
are crowded with people who are not seeking leisure but are running
away from it. The same is true of the compulsive worker, the man
who boasts of how little leisure he has, and who speeds himself
up until he explodes in neuroses and stomach ulcers.

We tend to think of leisure as having nothing in particular to do:
this is what the word means in Thorstein Veblen's *Theory of the
Leisure Class*, where he is examining the traditional idea of the
gentleman as the man who does not work. But even the old
leisure class did possess some essential social values—courtesy,
good taste, patronage of the arts—and a democracy has the problem
of trying to retain those genuine values, while making them
accessible to anyone. It is still true that liberal education is the
education of the free man, and has no meaning out of the context
of freedom. The really privileged person is not the man who has no
work to do, but the man who works freely, and has voluntarily assumed
his duties in the light of his conception of himself and his social
function. The underprivileged person is (at best) the servile worker,
or what Carlyle called the drudge, and every social advance, every
technological invention, every improvement in labour relations,
has the aim of reducing the amount of servile work in society.
But what makes free work free is its relation to the vision of life
that begins in the moment of leisure. The poet Yeats took as a motto

for one of his books the phrase "in dreams begin responsibilities."
It is also in man's dream of a humanized world that all learning,
art and science begin. As Aristotle pointed out, the words school and
scholarship come from *schole*, leisure. The Bible says that leisure is
the beginning of wisdom: it also says that fear of the Lord is the
beginning of wisdom, but the two statements are quite compatible,
for religion too has its origin in leisure. Christianity illustrated
this fact when it changed a day of rest at the end of the week into a
day of leisure at the beginning of the week. The university
illustrates the same principle, in its secular form, when it places
a four-year voluntary liberal education at the beginning of adult life.

We also tend to think of the rewards of leisure as individual possessions,
like the love of poetry or music that fills the spare intervals of our
lives with private moments of grace and beauty. But behind these
private possessions lies a social possession, a vision of life that we
share with others. This shared vision is the total form of art,
man's vision of a human world, to which every individual work of
art belongs. Most of us are seldom aware of the power of words
in forming the visions which hold society together. Special occasions,
like the familiar words spoken at marriages and funerals, or a
critical moment in history that we happen to live through,
like the summer of 1940 when the free world had practically nothing
but Churchill's prose style left to fight with, are usually all that
bring them to our minds.

Yet any newspaper can show us how society turns on the hinges
of words and numbers. The people who make fortunes out of
uranium stocks owe their wealth and social prestige to an
absent-minded professor, badly in need of a haircut, who scribbled
down $e = mc^2$ on a piece of paper fifty years ago. The biggest names
in the news at present, as far as space is concerned, are Eisenhower
and Krushchev, one a Republican and the other a Marxist. The
Republicans owe their existence to the fact that a century ago a
long-legged Illinois lawyer put a few words together that made up a
social vision for the American people of genuine dignity and power,
and so enabled the Republican party to stand for something.
Communism owes its existence to the fact that a century ago a
carbuncular political agitator disappeared into the British Museum to
write a sprawling, badly organized and grittily technical book on
capitalism, which even its author was unable to finish. I have no
doubt that the philosophy and economics of that work have been
refuted many times, but no refutation will have any effect on it.
Marxism is a vision of life, with its roots in the social imagination, and
it will endure, at least as a vision, until another of greater intensity
grows up in its place.

The people who run away from their own leisure will, of course, also run away from the articulate sounds of words that would recall them to their dreams and their responsibilities. Just as a frightened child may be reassured to hear the murmur of his parents' voices downstairs, so the childish in our society turn to the books and newspapers, the television programmes and the political leaders, that supply them with the endless, unmeaning babble of the lonely crowd. If you remember George Orwell's *1984*, you will recall the decisive role of "Newspeak" in that book. There is only one way to degrade mankind permanently, and that is to destroy language. The whole history of ordered public speech, from the Hebrew prophets who denounced their kings and the Demosthenes and Cicero who fought for the Classical republics down through Milton and Jefferson and Mill and Lincoln, has been inseparably a part of the heritage of freedom. In the nature of things—or rather in the nature of words—it cannot be otherwise. We naturally demand leadership from our leaders, but thugs and gangsters can give us leadership, of a kind: if we demand articulateness as well, we are demanding something that only a genuine vision of human life can provide.

In the near future the university of which Dr. Bissell is now president will have a steadily increasing flow of bright young people, eager to be directed toward maturity with the least loss of time. It may strike them as a trifle irrelevant that some of their teachers should be so concerned over their failure to understand the use of the comma. But it is precisely in such foxholes that the battle is fought out between clarity and confusion, between thought and prejudice, between the truth that makes free and the bumbling of the father of lies. If the governing providence of the world were to go to sleep, as Plato suggests that it does from time to time; if the self-destroying legion of devils in man were to break loose; if the world were reduced to a darkness without form and void—then we could only believe or hope that an eternally creative Word would still be there, commanding the light to shine again. The human word is neither immortal nor invulnerable; but it is the power that orders our chaos, and the light by which we live.

THE SCIENTIFIC STUDY OF VALUES*

by Clyde Kluckhohn, Professor of Anthropology,
Harvard University

T his afternoon I should like to consider with you four inter-related
topics:

1. A conception of values from the standpoint of behavioral science;
2. The case for the study of values, so defined;
3. Brief summary of some aspects, both empirical and theoretical, of a
research project upon values in five cultures;
4. Further exploration of the theory of values.

I.

In another place (C. Kluckhohn, 1951a) I have attempted a technical
and precise definition of values and value-orientations appropriate to
work in the behavioral sciences. Permit me here to speak more loosely
but still, I hope, communicating what I regard as essential. In the
broadest sense, behavioral scientists may usefully think of values as
abstract and perduring standards which are held by an individual
and/or a specified group to transcend the impulses of the moment and
ephemeral situations. From the psychological point of view, a value
may be defined as that aspect of motivation which is referable to
standards, personal or cultural, that do not arise solely out of an
immediate situation and the satisfaction of needs and primary drives.
Concretely, of course, values are always manifested in the verbal and
motor behavior of individuals. There are research purposes for which it
is necessary to focus upon personal values as such, though such
personal values are ordinarily no more than the idiosyncratic variants
of values which may, by abstraction, be attributed to a group or to a
culture or sub-culture. Henceforth in this paper I shall be speaking
solely of these cultural values.

A value is a selective orientation toward experience, implying deep
commitment or repudiation, which influences the "choice" between

*This paper is based upon work conducted for the project, Comparative
Studies of Value in Five Cultures, of the Laboratory of Social Relations,
Harvard University, and supported by the Rockefeller Foundation through its
Division of Social Sciences. Some later pages constitute a revision
of portions of Kluckhohn (1956) and gratitude is expressed to the
University of Chicago Press for this privilege.

possible alternatives in action. These orientations may be cognitive and expressed or merely inferable from recurrent trends in behavior.

A value, though conditioned by biological and social necessity, is in its specific form arbitrary or conventional. Values function as much in cultural definitions of the situation as do that culture's existential beliefs.

Behavior oriented by a value or by values does indeed constitute one class of preferential behavior. But such behavior belongs to the category regarded as "desirable" or "undesirable" by the group with which the individual identifies—not to that of acts which the individual simply desires or does not desire. Sometimes, to be sure, the two categories merge in the life experience of wise or fortunate individuals. You will remember the saying attributed to Confucius: "In my old age I found that I had to do what I wanted to do and wanted to do what I had to do." Nevertheless both introspection and observation tell us forcefully that the areas of "the desirable" and "the desired" are not always—or even often—exactly coextensive.

This circumstance sometimes escapes behavioral scientists. When I talk to clinical psychologists they frequently say "Oh, yes, I know what you mean by 'value.' It is what we call 'need' or 'cathexis.' " And the experimental psychologists will similarly remark "That is what we refer to as 'drive strength.' " If this equation of concepts were adequate to our data, we should—on the principle of Occam's razor—simply drop the term, "value." Yet it is an induction from ordinary experience that, on occasion, all of us behave in ways that go contrary, in whole or in part, to our "wants" or "desires" as they arise in the biological organism at that moment. The existence of the value-element may transform the desired into the not-desired or the ambivalently desired. Disvalued activity is constantly cathected. A cathexis is an impulse. A value or values restrain or canalize impulses in terms of what a group has defined as wider or more enduring goods. The "desirable" becomes a distinctive component in motivation. The uniqueness of the presence of values, a somewhat separate, special area in human life, different in kind from other cognitive and affective influences, is almost universally recognized or "felt" as such.

"Needs," for instance, and "values" certainly have mutual implications. The few elemental needs that all human beings share undoubtedly have a recognizable similarity in all cultures, though differently weighted and varyingly formulated in detail. On the other hand, some needs (for example for food and water) are merely biological givens. The question of value arises only when the possibility of selection in accord with abstract standards exists or is held to exist. When certain desired and nutritious foods are tabooed or when others are arbitrarily considered "better," then and only then are we in the realm of value. "Values" designate preferences that cannot be derived solely from the existence of needs. Some "choices" do not involve value elements but only need elements. Specific bodily deprivations and gratifications may be relevant to a great many values but do not themselves constitute value phenomena. Needs and values are not thereby identified. Moreover, their relationship may be circular. Psychological needs are created by cultural values; it remains true that some values are responses to basic human needs.

II.

Values, then, are images formulating positive or negative action commitments. They take distinctive forms in different cultures, tend to persist tenaciously through time, and are not mere random outcomes of conflicting human desires. They are standards which complicate the individual's satisfaction of his immediate wishes and needs. Can they be studied scientifically? (I assume that the concept, "science," designates a method and a point of view rather than any particular body of content.)

Until quite recently behavioral scientists have been shy about using the category, "value." The term had an important place in the conceptual reportory of economics but was technically defined in a sense only remotely related to the meaning I have proposed. Psychologists, sociologists, and anthropologists avoided the word. They necessarily sometimes described value phenomena but under such rubrics as "primitive religion," "aesthetics," or even "ethics." This was largely, I believe, because these disciplines were struggling to establish themselves as "sciences." And the prevailing fashion in science insisted that science dealt only with "facts" or with "facts in a conceptual scheme." "Values" were the exclusive province of theologians, philosophers, and humanists. Many scientists frankly treated values as verbal rationalizations or epiphenomena—at least from the standpoint of "true" science. This was partly on the valid ground that until a decade or two ago physiology and neurology declared themselves unable to discover a structural-functional basis in the human nervous system for the influence of *any* general ideas upon conduct. Also, "values" were too close to "purpose," and it was dogma that science could have nothing to do with "purpose" but only with "motivation." In accord with the great scientific tradition of sticking to the "tangible" or observable, one major approach was that of stimulus-response psychology which produced a learning theory built upon "drives," the physiological bases of which were presumed to be known or discoverable. The psychoanalytic psychiatrists, on the other hand, followed by many clinical psychologists and anthropologists, took the Freudian lead in dealing almost entirely with unconscious and irrational factors in motivation.

In sum, the doctrine of Kant, Rickert, Windelband, and Dilthey that there were realms of fact and realms of value and that investigations of these two realms could be mingled only at peril to the orderliness of each prevailed for a long time. It was considered irresponsible and actually "unscientific" by definition for anyone who called himself a scientist to deal with matters of value. A landmark in the reaction was the presidential address to the American Association for the Advancement of Science in 1936 by the psychologist, E. L. Thorndike. A few years later another well-known psychologist, Wolfgang Köhler, published a book entitled *The Place of Value in a World of Facts.* At about the same time the British anthropologist, E. E. Evans-Pritchard, unashamedly made frequent use of the concept in a monograph on an African tribe, the Nuer. So far as I have been able to discover, however, it was 1948 before values were explicitly and systematically treated in a textbook on anthropology. Nevertheless, during the past fifteen years, sociologists, psychologists, and anthropologists have been publishing numerous empirical and theoretical studies concerning values.

Ironically enough, just as for long behavioral scientists eschewed values because they aspired to be "scientists," so they now give their attention to values because they are convinced that this is essential to a science of human behavior. Essential, since the most distinctive thing about man is that he is the valuing animal and values often influence his courses of action and occasionally are decisive. In the case of anthropology the matter seems quite clear. Just as the essence of culture is patterned selectivity, so this selectivity can be understood only in terms of the value system. Any behavior influenced by culture is an historically created, discriminating way of responding. From the anthropological standpoint, it would almost be a definition of values to say: "Those features of a culture that are so pivotal as regards its distinctiveness that one can detect their ubiquity and trace their shaping of widely varied sectors of cultural content." The "inner order" of a culture rests upon its peculiar existential and evaluative concepts and images—and their linkages and weightings.

My own general position accords with that expressed this year by the famous geneticist, H. J. Muller: " . . . values are as legitimate a subject of scientific investigation as any other phenomena pertaining to living beings." Elsewhere (C. Kluckhohn, 1958) I have discussed briefly the question as to whether science can say something about instrumental values as appraised in terms of their relative efficacy as means to designated ends. I have even ventured to say something about the far more difficult question as to whether science can contribute to an objective appraisal of competing or contradictory ultimate values. Today, however, I propose to take only the minimal position already developed by Machiavelli, Nietzsche, and other writers. Namely, we do not need to beg the issue as to whether or not the "truth" of value-judgments can be scientifically determined in order to take a firm stand that: (a) values can be described with some precision; and (b) their place in the structure of the culture and the workings of the society can be established.

In other words, I assert here only that values are cultural and psychological facts of a certain type which can be discovered with as much detachment as other types of cultural and psychological facts. Fundamentally, one does the same as in other areas of behavior: one listens to what people say and for what they fail to say; one observes what they do and don't do; one gets at what they are unable or unwilling to say by projective tests, "depth interviews," and other techniques.

III.

Permit me to tell you something about one attempt to put into practice the theoretical position just stated. During the years 1949–1954 the Laboratory of Social Relations of Harvard University, supported by a grant from the Rockefeller Foundation, did research among five culturally distinct groups in New Mexico. Field work was carried out by some forty investigators from Harvard and nine other universities. Since questions of culture (anthropology), social structure (sociology), the psychology of groups (social psychology, and individual motivation (clinical psychology) are all inextricably interwoven in the area of values, there were field workers from each of these disciplines. An historian, a political scientist, and two philosophers also participated.

The initial conception of the project was summarized as follows (C. Kluckhohn, 1951b, p. viii):

Five distinct cultures co-exist in the same relatively small ecological area in New Mexico. For two full generations four of the groups involved have been in continued face-to-face contact. They have also been subject to approximately the same historical process, influenced by the same streams of cultural diffusion. The number of individuals in each cultural group is small enough to permit convincing workmanship in detail with relatively small resources in personnel. All five societies must meet the problems of gaining subsistence under environmental conditions which present the same challenge and hazards to all groups. Today, all of these societies have available essentially the same technology.
The research design is premised upon the possibility of using the methods of agreement and difference (and of replication) in five

different life-ways co-existing in the same external environment.
Some of the same values are probably current in all five groups,
perhaps even held by a majority of the members of each group.
The degree to which this is true can be settled only by intensive
and systematic investigation. Demonstration of similar values would
have important theoretical implications. Likewise, the extent of
variation among values held by individuals within a group has never,
to our knowledge, been carefully described. Finally, the fact that some
values continue to be distinctive of each separate culture, in spite
of the common environmental setting and historical contact, requires
explanation.
Each group will be studied in terms of its own internal mechanisms.
For example, how does each group handle the scapegoat problem?
The non-Indian groups (and the Indian to an increasing extent)
export their young men to urban areas. How are the pressures handled
in these altered situations? To what extent do the original values
persist after protracted residence away?

Some Primary Questions:
1. What values characterize the five distinct cultures in this area?
2. What is the place of each value system in the total structural-
functional economy of each culture?
3. By what processes of formal and informal teaching and learning
are the value systems perpetuated in each culture?
4. What changes in value have occurred (a) in the period for which
satisfactory documentation is available? (b) in the period of
the project?
5. In terms of what situational pressures have such changes
occurred? In what ways has each group reacted differently to roughly
similar pressures because of (a) different cultural traditions,
(b) different social structures?
6. To what extent is the range and incidence of distinct personality
types various for the five cultural groups? If such variation exists,
what is its relation to the perpetuation of the several value systems,
the resistance of each to change, the distinctive patterning of the
changes which are occurring in each culture?
7. What do value systems mean to individuals in each group?
8. To some degree each of the above-listed questions is merely a
special phase of a more general problem:
Why do different value systems continue to exist in five cultures all
having to meet similar problems of adjustment and survival in
the same ecological area, all having been exposed by actual contact and
by stimulus diffusion to each other's value ideas and practices?

Needless to say, we did not obtain adequate answers to all of these
questions, though it is fair to report that we did get some illumination

upon them all. Much of the actual research procedure could best be characterized as a series of "fishing expeditions." We did not try to force each worker to take up a given item in the outline for the investigation. Individuals were almost completely free to do what they were interested in so long as they convinced those in charge of the project that their topic was plausibly related to values. Investigators *were* asked to pay particular attention to certain "operational indices," of which the following are representative:

1. Manifestations of approval or disapproval in word or deed.
2. Differential effort exhibited toward the attainment of ends, access to means, or acquisition of modes of behavior.
3. Behavior (and hypothetical behavior) in "choice" and especially crisis situations.

Empirical studies ranged from cross-cultural interviewing and observation on nausea to the use of a tachistoscope to discover whether perception of closure varied culturally to child play with "projective" toys and drawings; from social history and humor to the aesthetics of music and the graphic arts. Some research, to be sure, was more squarely within the framework of values as traditionally conceived: a comparison of the values of Navahos who had served in World War II with those of their close relatives of about the same age who had not had this experience; an analysis of myths which dissected out relationships between values, social organization and other variables; an enquiry by interview into the tacit premises of an ethical system; an analysis of Zuni quarrels and "legal" cases in value terms. On the assumption that abundant observation must precede significant experimentation, we did only a few small studies that could be described as "experiments" in the strict sense. However, some investigations—one of which I shall speak about at greater length presently—did have tight research designs. But the dominant tone of the Values Project as a whole, was, deliberately, "loose" rather than "tight" in conception. This we felt to be proper in a field which had been but little explored empirically. One needs to "go on fishing expeditions," that is, to uncover the phenomena in their range and variety before one can proceed to a rigor that is not premature and hence false or distorting.

Fifteen books and monographs have appeared. Some of these are devoted to describing the five value systems, while others are comparative examinations of topical areas. The hundred or more papers arising out of this project deal with method and technique, theory, as well as reports of facts and their interconnections. I believe that any competent student of this literature would assent to my proposition that reliable and valid models of value systems *can* be constructed on the basis of empirical data, even though he would quite correctly add that some of this work reveals incompleteness, imprecision, and crudity. The work of analysis and synthesis is still proceeding. It will be another decade before publication ceases. Within eighteen months there will appear a one-volume summary of empirical findings. Two or three years later we shall publish another summary volume which centers on theory.

Out of our rather massive storehouse I can only select for quick review by way of illustration two investigations which were productive both factually and theoretically. One cannot satisfactorily describe or compare cultural value-systems until one has identified the constituent elements. This task was effectively performed by the philosopher-anthropologist, Ethel Albert. (Albert, 1956.)

Dr. Albert delimits as elements of all value systems five categories in descending order of generality:

1. *Value premises* are defined as the most general conceptions of desirable and undesirable modes, means, and ends of action. They include the place of human beings in the scheme of things, e.g. as lower than the angels, higher animals, or pawns of fate; the temporal direction and significance of human history; beliefs about "the meaning of life" and the nature of happiness; conceptions of moral worth, e.g. as dependent on right action or good intentions, self-interest or social welfare; definitions of "good" and "bad," "right," and "wrong"—in short, the "first principles" of conduct. . . .
2. As one examines in detail numerous specific values, it becomes increasingly clear that values cluster about a limited number of cores. These *"focal"* values have a dual status; they are inferable from groupings of values, but at the same time are explicitly valued within a culture and recourse had to them to justify and explain (presumably) less central values. Knowledge, family, possessions, enjoyment, and health are focal values for the Navaho. Work, health, education, and recreation have a similar place in the Mormon value system, and for the Texan homesteaders, individualism, personal success and community progress are focal. . . .
3. *Directives* comprise the prescriptions and prohibitions . . . of a society. They include laws, commandments, rules of conduct, taboos, obligations and duties, rights and privileges, and any other rules or standards which are intended to regulate conduct. . . .
4. *Character* refers to the "virtues" and "vices", the qualities of personality which are approved or disapproved, encouraged or suppressed, rewarded or punished . . .
5. *Valued and disvalued entities* comprise the numerous and varied objects, feeling states, situations, and activities at the lowest level of generality in the value system. . . .

Let us now, for more concreteness, consider some examples from the five cultures studied. Dr. Albert states the *value premises* of the culture of the Zuni Indians as follows:

1. Harmonious order, construed as control and integration of all beings, is the greatest good and primary moral imperative.
2. Rigid correctness, formalism and constant human activity are required to achieve the good life.
3. Zuni is the focus of human and supernatural interest.
4. Good and bad are sharply differentiated; the former sacred, the latter belonging to witchcraft, with some activities neutral. Evil is not to be tolerated but transmuted or destroyed.
5. Moderation is required in all activities.

Contrast and compare the value premises of the nearby Spanish-Americans:

1. The persons of the universe are inherently moral, hierarchially ordered, voluntaristically motivated.
2. Whatever happens is the will of God, but men must obey the divine commandments.
3. Man is weak and sinful but has knowledge of right and wrong.
4. Rewards and punishments are attached to human actions.
5. Salvation is hoped for in the afterlife; the good life on earth is a complex of contrasting elements, unified by aesthetic-emotive appreciation.
6. Good and evil are ever-present, conflicting forces, beyond human control but affecting human well-being.

Examples have already been given of *focal values*. Here are Texan "Homesteader" *directives*, then those of the Navaho:

1. Conduct should be governed by principles of common decency.
2. Do as you please, provided you don't hurt anyone or interfere with the rights of others.
3. "Do unto others as you would be done by," considering the desirability of minding your own business and looking after yourself.
4. Be persistent, be willing to take a chance, but stay within the rules of the game.
5. In social and personal relations, be a good sport, live and let live, help people who are in trouble.
6. "Don't go back on your raising."

Navaho:

1. Maintain orderliness.
a. All things are to be done as tradition prescribes.
b. Behave decorously in all situations in order to avoid illness, poverty, gossip, etc.

c. For self-development, familial solidarity and community respect: work hard; learn things; think before you act; take care of your property; take care of your mental and physical health and appearance.
2. Avoid or neutralize strange or dangerous situations.
3. Get along well with everyone, relatives especially.

Some of the *character* values of the Mormons are: outgoing warmth and community pride; purity of mind and body; effort and strength; faith in Mormonism. Good persons, of either sex and at any age, are those who approximate closely the idea of the Saint, manifesting in word and deed: obedience, love, respect, industriousness, co-operativeness, responsibility, moral-religious righteousness and joy. A comparable list for the Spanish-Americans includes the friendly helpfulness of neighbors, the bravery and sexual potency of men, faithfulness to the Church and adherence to customs. The good father is loving, industrious, responsible, serious, thrifty, competent to look after his family, a strict disciplinarian. A good woman is pure, religious, obedient to her husband, fertile, a good housekeeper, moral mainstay of her home. Good children are respectful of their elders, loving and solicitous toward them.

Finally, let us consider some of the most prominent valued entities in each culture:

Navaho: material and non-material goods; skills, secular and ceremonial; fertility and productivity; mobility; sociability; sensual pleasures.
Zuni: ceremonial and economic property; objects and skills related to entertainment, beauty, humor, fertility and rain; the town of Zuni: its houses, people, and customs.
Spanish-American: material objects necessary for survival; religious and magical objects and techniques, for times of trouble; beautiful objects and exciting experiences; enjoyment, religion; custom; family; hope, faith, and love.
Mormon: material goods: the village, its church, school, stores, and dwellings, the village dam, farming and grazing land, cattle, horses, and mechanical devises; recreation; theological knowledge; technical and argicultural abilities; thoughts, feelings, and actions proper to a Mormon.
Texans: land, machines, and seed; strength and health of mind and body; dancing; loafing.

The second investigation from which I wish to present you a few aspects involves a theory of value orientations which emphasizes the "built-in" variation in each value system and a methodology for ascertaining the value-profile of each culture and for comparing in rigorously standardized ways different value profiles and

their internal variations. (F. Kluckhohn and Strodtbeck, 1959.)
Florence Kluckhohn's theory of value orientations singles out five
crucial questions common to all human groups:

1. What is the character of innate human nature? (Human-Nature
Orientation)
2. What is the relation of man to nature (supernature)?
(Man-Nature Orientation)
3. What is the temporal focus of human life? (Time Orientation)
4. What is the modality of human activity? (Activity Orientation)
5. What is the modality of man's relationship to other men?
(Relational Orientation).

In detail, a wide continuum of cultural "answers" to these questions
exists. Nevertheless there are also, abstractly, certain recurrent and
characteristic types of response which are schematized in the following
diagram:

	Evil	Neutral	Mixture of Good & Evil	Good
Innate Human Nature	Mutable-Immutable	Mutable-Immutable		Mutable-Immutable
Man's relation to Nature & Supernature	Subjugation to Nature	Harmony with Nature		Mastery over Nature
Time Focus	Past	Present		Future
Modality of Human Activity	Being	Being-in-Becoming		Doing
Modality of Man's Relationship to Other Men	Lineal	Collateral		Individualistic

NOTE: Since each of the orientations is considered to be independently variable,
the arrangement in columns of sets of orientations is only the accidental result
of this particular diagram. All combinations are considered to be possible. For
example, a Doing Activity orientation may be combined with a Mastery-over-
Nature position and Individualism as it is in dominant American culture, or,
as one finds in Navaho Indian Culture, it may be in combination with a first
order Harmony-with-Nature position and Collaterality.

Perhaps the greatest theoretical innovation in Florence Kluckhohn's
work upon value orientations is that her theory permits—indeed
demands—a multi-dimensional analysis. Previous characterizations of
core values were too static, too absolutistic, took far too little account
of variation. Thus for Ruth Benedict Zuni culture was "Apollonian"
and Kwakiutl culture was "Dionysian." Such sweeping labels are,
at best, very rough impressionistic catch-alls. They ignore the
counter-currents. All ethnographers know, for example, that there
are at Zuni patterned behaviors which, in Benedict's own terms,
are unmistakably "Dionysian." These she either fails to mention

or, in effect, tries to explain away. Moreover, Benedict largely fails to take account of the fact that cultural values are varyingly weighted in different kinds of activities and for persons occupying particular statuses or playing particular roles.

Florence Kluckhohn, on the other hand, postulates systematic variation in the whole realm of cultural phenomena and not least in the value sector. There is both permitted and required variation. As regards the value of orientations specifically, she assumes that each of the three positions for the five orientations will be represented in every culture. What needs to be determined is the rank ordering. Spanish-Americans, for instance, were found to have these profiles of rank orders:

Relational:	1. Individualistic	2. Lineal	3. Collateral
Time:	1. Present	2. Future	3. Past
Man-Nature:	1. Subjugated	2. Over-nature	3. With-nature

The profile of rank orders for the same value orientations of the Texan neighbors of the Spanish-American village comes out this way:

Relational:	1. Individualistic	2. Collateral	3. Lineal
Time:	1. Future	2. Present	3. Past
Man-Nature:	1. Over	2. With	3. Subjugated

As a matter of fact, the detailed statistical anlaysis of F. Kluckhohn and Strodtbeck reveals still finer shadings. Thus they demonstrate that the Spanish-Americans are only *slightly* more individualistically than lineally oriented in their dominant position for the relational value orientation.

In any case, it is quite evident that a comparison in terms of profiles is immensely more just to the rich variability of actuality— *and* to the essential nature of value systems—than to rest with saying: "Spanish-Americans are individualistic, present-time oriented, and regard themselves as subjugated to nature, whereas Texans are individualistic, future-oriented, and intent upon mastering nature." The contrasts in the various second- and third-order positions in each case sensitively reveal important information. One hardly needs belabor the advantages of the profiles versus single portmanteau words such as "Dionysian" or "Apollonian."

Another outstanding feature of the theory which I can only mention and not do justice to here is a new outlook which it provides for a model of value change and of cultural change generally. There is that sort of change summed up in Desmoulins' phrase: "Plus ça change, plus c'est la même chose." It is likewise generally recognized that fundamental values alter slowly—in the overwhelming majority of cases. But—and this is the new point—basic value shifts occur when external pressures impinge upon the already existent variation in the system. The systematic variation always contains the potentiality for change but remains dormant or latent* until environmental events or intensified contacts with other cultures bring a second- or third-order position into dominance. If this be correct, we escape the puzzling *mystique* of "immanent causation." My wife had studied the values of the Spanish-American village fifteen years before the field work of the Values Project was carried out. At this time the lineal orientation was definitely dominant. By 1951 it had become, by a shade, subordinate to the individualistic orientation. This shift she had predicted in 1936 and specified the variant individuals who would be the bearers of the trend.

The F. Kluckhohn-Strodtbeck book makes a methodical contribution which is as noteworthy as it is theoretical. An instrument (a schedule of alternative choices which were derived from the value orientation theory) was devised to test the differences and similarities of value orientations in the five cultures. The full schedule contained series of three to five sets of such alternative choices. The instrument was administered in the native languages to random samples of adult informants from each culture. Let me illustrate in the concrete by item 1 in the schedule on the relational orientation. Informants were told:

When a community has to make arrangements for water, such as drill a well, there are three different ways they can decide to arrange things like location, and who is going to do the work:
(Lineal) A. There are some communities where it is mainly the older or recognized leaders of the important families who decide the plans. Everyone usually accepts what they say without much discussion since they are the ones who are used to deciding such things and are the ones who have had the most experience.
(Collateral) B. There are some communities where most people in the group have a part in making the plans. Lots of different people talk, but nothing is done until *almost* everyone comes to agree as to what is best to be done.
(Individualistic) C. There are some communities where everyone holds to his own opinion, and they decide the matter by vote. They do what the largest number want even though there are still a very great many people who disagree and object to the action.

*"Dormant or latent" only from the point of view of leading to value shifts. When a society and its value system are in a state of equilibrium the variant values are active but mainly supportive of the dominant values.

WHICH WAY DO YOU THINK IS USUALLY BEST IN SUCH
CASES?
WHICH OF THE OTHER TWO WAYS DO YOU THINK IS
BETTER?
WHICH WAY OF ALL THREE WAYS DO YOU THINK MOST
OTHER PERSONS IN ——— WOULD THINK IS USUALLY
BEST?

Great care was taken in developing the schedule to base the
questions upon experiences and dilemmas common to all five
cultures. The responses were analyzed by Dr. Strodtbeck's modification
of the Kendall rank order technique to determine the differences
statistically significant both within and between cultures. Also, the
findings were used to test the validity of predictions made in
advance by "experts" on each culture. On the whole, these
predictions stood up very well. But much new information was
provided and many new questions were posed that demand empirical
study. To participants in the Values Project perhaps the most
impressive thing about the work of F. Kluckhohn and Strodtbeck was
the economy of effort with which data and interpretation could
be obtained by this standardized effort that fitted beautifully with
conclusions firmly reached by other methods—but which had
been far more costly in time.

IV.

Finally, I want to sketch for you another approach which is far less
thoroughly worked through both empirically and theoretically
than the one we have just been considering. Yet I think it to be
promising both as a supplement to the other line of attack and
perhaps also as posing issues which, while overlapping, are somewhat
wider and somewhat different. The two approaches share many points
of departure, but this one arises immediately out of anthropological
linguistics and does not rely at all upon statistical manipulations.
It is a form of pattern analysis, a trial at transferring to value-culture
some procedures which have been applied with great success
to linguistic culture.

A short historical digression may be worthwhile. I believe that the
affiliation of cultural anthropologists for pattern analysis has
comparatively simple roots. In the first place, the field situation
forced them to realize that the acts and thoughts of men and women
do not remain dammed up in the neat little pools which the
Western academic tradition has labeled "religion," "economics,"
and the like. They saw, with Dostoevsky, that:

Reality is a thing of infinite diversity, and defies the most
ingenious deductions and definitions of abstract thought,

nay, abhors the clear and precise classifications we delight in:
Reality tends to infinite subdivisions of things, and truth is a
matter of infinite shadings and differentiations.

At the same time, their unavoidable experience with the ramified
context and with abrupt alternations from one configuration to
another compelled anthropologists to see that form and structure
pervade human behavior and human cultures as much as they do
molecules or crystals or organisms, and that the crucial structure
points of one culture differ from those of another just as the planes
of cleavage of one kind of crystal distinguish these from others,
even others which to the eye appear rather similar.

Anthropological emphasis upon pattern and structure is, of course,
unique only as regards intensity and certain details. In many ways, it is
very similar to the approach used by sophisticated students of
art styles. All behavioral scientists must necessarily face problems
of pattern analysis, and form is a central theme in almost all of the
sciences at mid-twentieth century. But the distinctive aspects of the
anthropological outlook derive primarily from the second historical
factor: among behavorial scientists, only cultural anthropologists
have been in sustained contact with the extraordinary developments
in structural linguistics over the past generation. This resulted—as
so many things do—from a series of historical accidents.
Comparative studies of culture really date from the discovery that
Sanscrit was related to Greek and Latin. This finding was dramatic
in the contemporary intellectual climate, partly because it cast
doubt upon the customary assumption that Hebrew had been the
original language of mankind. At any rate, the development of
comparative Indo-European philology gave a tremendous impetus to
many kinds of comparative investigation of which cultural
anthropology was one. From its very beginnings, then, cultural
anthropology had a kind of persistent tie to linguistics, and the
sub-culture of the profession prescribed that the anthropologist
would concern himself with the languages of the peoples he studied.

The philologists, however, showed little disposition to investigate
the structures of "primitive" languages. They devoted their efforts first
and foremost to the Indo-European tongues and, somewhat later,
to the comparative philology of Semitic languages and those of the
high civilization of the Far East. Students trained in philology
who did work with language families other than those just named
had a strong propensity to force the data into the Procrustean
bed of Indo-European phonological, grammatical, and syntactical
categories. Anthropologists, and notably Franz Boaz, speedily
became aware that this brought about a ludicrous distortion of the
materials. Boas forcefully argued that the first principle was that

features both of sound and of morphology had to be seen "from within" i.e., in terms of the principles governing the system in which they occurred in nature.

The insights of Boas were carried further by Edward Sapir who was equally brilliant as linguist and as anthropologist. A series of papers by Sapir such as "Sound Patterns in Language" and "The Unconscious Patterning of Behavior in Society" had a profound impact upon cultural anthropologists and especially upon such "configurationalists" as Ruth Benedict. Sapir pointed out " . . . the naive Frenchman confounds the two sounds 's' of 'sick' and 'th' of 'thick' in a single pattern point—not because he is really unable to hear the difference, but because the setting up of such a difference disturbs his feeling for the necessary configuration of linguistic sounds." This statement constitutes a miniscule paradigm for a whole theory. What is often decisive in the realms of culture (of which language is one) is not so and so much of something or whether or not phenomena have a random distribution (cultural phenomena, by definition, have other than a chance distribution) but rather the question of order and arrangement.

Moreover, a parsimonious description becomes possible only if the ordering principles are discovered. Speakers of English make sounds in which their vocal chords vibrate and others in which they do not. They also frequently make sounds which are—from the standpoint of an acoustics engineer—intermediate in type. However, the discrimination of shadings in this latter category is meaningless so far as language and culture are concerned, though it may have some interest for the biology or physics of speech sounds. The significant contrast in English is between voiced and voiceless, and this contrast is used to make many distinctions vital to communication in that language. In the Algonquin Indian tongues, on the other hand, it is a matter indifferent to communication whether the stop series of sounds are voiced, voiceless, or intermediate. Every language employs between about five and eleven decisive contrasts which determine the discriminations between various classes of sounds. Exactly the same kind of thing applies in another realm of culture, kinship systems. As Radcliffe-Brown has written:

We can "find" beneath the diversities, a limited number of general principles applied and combined in various ways.

Mead says:

In dealing with culture, the anthropologist makes the same assumptions about the rest of culture that the linguist makes about the language—that he is dealing with a system which can be delineated by analysis of a small number of very highly specified samples.

There is no doubt that anthropologists must supply more quantitative data and become more sophisticated in mathematical analysis. And yet there is no necessary connection between measure and structure. For culture in general, there are many indications that one of its aspects (language) constitutes the best model.

As Warren Weaver pointed out, seventeenth-century science dealt largely with problems of organized simplicity and nineteenth century science with problems of disorganized complexity where statistical techniques are most appropriate. But the crucial problems of present science generally are those of organized complexity. This is certainly true of anthropology, as Bateson says:

Another peculiarity of the data collected by cultural anthropologists is the extreme complexity of each individual datum. The requirement that each datum include full identification of the individual and description of the context is perhaps never fully met in practice. The fact remains, however, that a very large number of circumstances are always relevant, in the sense that a small change in any one of them might reverse, or drastically change, the form of the behavior which we are recording. There is, therefore, almost no possibility of handling the data statistically. The contexts, the individuals, and the behaviors are too various for their combinations and permutations to be handled in this way.

In my opinion, the study of cultural phenomena will progress mainly along linguistic lines by distinguishing contrastive categories— rather than by measurement as such. We cannot master our knowledge until we have objectified it, and we cannot objectify it until we have found conventions to give it form. What is necessary is to discover the determinate organizations of various clusters of cultural features: an exactness and constancy of relationship irrespective of content and dimensions. The indispensable criterion is that of linguistics: significant discontinuities. The naive adherents of "scientism" are actually disregarding the history of science which records that advance follows upon the isolation of the significant configurations. If operations are firmly and explicitly specified, "qualitative" judgments can be as systematic and as rigorous as quantitative ones. Moreover, as Edgar Anderson reminds us:

Biology has advanced most rapidly when appropriate qualitative measures have been developed and used with precision. In genetics, for example, the fundamental data are qualitative. Once obtained they are treated with such precision that most geneticists probably think of their work as purely quantitative. But the fundamental categories, "vestigial" vs. "non-vestigial," "scute" vs. "non-scute," "forked" vs. "non-forked," etc. are quite as qualitative as the fundamental categories of taxonomy . . . If the methods of Drosophila genetics were purely quantitative, the flies would not be classified in qualitative categories but their wing lengths, eye diameters, etc. would be laboriously measured. Imagine the difficulties of conducting a Drosophila experiment in which the only available data were the lengths and breadths of the wings! Genetics has been able to advance because it was willing to take the Mendelian recessive (a qualitative unit about whose ultimate significance relatively little was known) and to use that unknown but recognizable entity as a basic unit.

Recent investigations by Anderson represent, I believe, a dramatic warning to behavioral scientists who wish to measure without isolating elementary entities based upon significant discontinuities. Graphic representation of a few carefully selected features enabled biologists and many non-biologists to differentiate two species correctly, even when they were not told the number of species involved. In contrast, analysis of variance and regression techniques yielded inconclusive or much less efficient results. He comments:

If one sets out to analyze the difference between two species, the actual data are individual plants or animals, each individual a mutiple-sense-impression of size, shape, color, texture, etc. . . . To analyze the nature of these differences we need to make a selection among the thousands of sense-impressions which come to us from each specimen . . . the two species may be completely separated by the resultant of seven variables even though any single variable would not suffice when used singly. . . . An impressive proportion of the multiple sense impressions, such as differences between species or varieties, where from each individual a seemingly infinite number of numerical facts could be derived . . . the customary methods of biometry are still inappropriate and ineffective. . . . Pointer readings are not more exact than any other kind of precise record . . . species are differentiated by combinations of characters more certainly than by single characters. . . .

It will have been noted that in speaking of genetics, Anderson referred to a number of complementary categories ("forked" vs. "non-forked," etc.). Similarly, linguists in their elegant analyses of one aspect of culture have found it extremely useful to set up a series of distinctive contrasts or oppositions, usually binary, which serve to identify each separate phoneme (sound class distinctive in that language). A "lump" or "bundle" of such "distinctive features" defines a phoneme. In its simplest form, the process is like a specialized version of the "twenty questions game." Thus one may ask, "Is the phoneme vocalic? Yes or no? In Russian, eleven such questions will identify each phoneme uniquely. In the French phonemic system, the binary oppositions are the following: vowel-consonant, nasal-oral, saturated-diluted, grave-acute, tense-lax, and continuous-intercepted. While the particular principles or distinctive features and their combinations vary from one phonemic system to another, a total list of the oppositions utilized in known languages would not exceed twenty.

There are grounds, both empirical and theoretical, for supposing that a similar approach will yield good results with other aspects of culture, including cultural values. Human nature and the human situation are such that there are some fundamental questions of value upon which all cultures have felt compelled to take a position, explicit or implicit. As in the case of language, the foci or structure-points are largely supplied by the limits and potentialities given by the physical world, human biology, and social requirements. With language, the properties of sound waves, the anatomy and physiology of the speech organs, and social (communicative) needs constrain the range of variation. With values, such unavoidable facts as dependence upon the external environment, birth and death, and social relatedness make value "choices" in these areas inescapable. Nor here again is the range of loci for selection or indeed of possible selections at each locus unconstrained. Just as all phonemic systems include nasals, stops, and sibilants, so all value systems place their weightings, for instance, on the desirable relations to nature, other individuals, and the self within a describable set of alternatives.

The entities of value-culture may not have the all-or-none character of a simple physical event like the phones found in language culture. Rather, they may have the character of weightings or emphases that are, one the whole, dominant in the culture. Even here there are parallels. A language or a phonemic system is, after all, a high order abstraction. Concretely, each person's speech is an idiodialect, and even this varies through time and between situations. Similarly, some individuals or groups may accept the variant rather than the dominant cultural values. They may reject some or many of the core values. To those values, whether dominant or variant, that they do accept each individual gives an interpretation and a coloring that is more or less private. It nevertheless remains meaningful to abstract common elements both in language and in values.

By proceeding as the geneticists have done so successfully with qualitative binary oppositions that represent significant discontinuities and by using the linguistic technique of seeing which distributions are complementary, coincident, incorporating and overlapping, anthropologists may be able to answer the questions that are at the heart of the principles of selectivity which determine the distinctiveness of each culture. Which combinations of value-emphases

are "impossible?" which are very rare and probably due to exceptional circumstances? which are so frequent as to be predictable? on which is no guess justified one way or the other? This particular task will indeed involve counting, but the initial determination of the contrasting pairs is more likely to follow the linguistic experience. Once a linguist is certain that in one instance a glottalized and a non-glottalized voiceless stop at the same articulatory position are in complementary distribution—or produce variation in the meaning of a morpheme—he knows he has two distinct phonemes.
In addition, he knows that there is an overwhelming likelihood that glottalization is one of the distinctive features of that language and is decisive in a number of phonemic contrasts.

Dichotomies are very slippery, to be sure, and the use of them often brings about a false simplification of the phenomena. Yet they are not merely convenient. The fact that human beings have two eyes, two hands, two feet; the alternation of night and day; the existence of two sexes, and other circumstances make it almost inevitable that people tend strongly to think in terms of "either . . . or" and "yes or no." In every culture there are many paired opposites: "love and hate," "friends and enemies," and the like. Hence, however false to the complexity of the natural world this anthropocentric two-valued logic may be, it remains true that human behavior frequently takes place on the binary basis, and this propensity introduces some regularities useful for scientific analysis. No multi-valued logic has thus far been very successful except at the level of formal mathematical notation.

In working out a first approximation (Kluckhohn, 1956) of suggested "distinctive features" of cross-cultural core value-emphases, I did not hesitate to draw upon the broadest categories of human experience as revealed in history, philosophy, categories of human experience as revealed in history, philosophy, and the arts. In my opinion, most recent anthropology has been too timid about resorting to general experience. There is assuredly a need for severely technical description and analysis. But there is equally in some contexts a necessity for breadth and sweep. The resultant first approximations can later be subjected to precise and refined scrutiny. Likewise, I did not hesitate to employ ordinary language. I am much less than satisfied with the terms I used. I feel that their denotations are fairly adequate, but the connotations evoked by English words (or words of any other single language) introduce elements of equivocation. Nevertheless, as a preliminary step, I think this alternative is preferable to the proposal of neologisms.

Cluster 1: MAN AND NATURE. These emphases are, in the first instance, existential rather than evaluative, but, as Northrop and others have argued, basic values are always tied to and dependent upon a culture's conception of the ultimate nature of things. All fundamental views of nature have implications for the total value system.

1a. Determinate-Indeterminate. This contrast hinges upon the priority given to orderliness (lawfulness) in the universe as opposed to chance or caprice or any factor or factors that make prediction or control impossible *in principle.* A "mechanistic" emphasis does not necessarily make human effort, including ritual effort, irrelevant. On the contrary, as the cases of Navaho, Zuni, and many other non-literate cultures show, this conception may heighten the amount and detail of ritual behavior, both negative and positive. The Epicurean and Buddhist instances show in other ways how this contrast is not that between theism and atheism. Nor is this exclusively the polarity between "fatalism" or "predetermination" versus "free will" or "accident." Rather, the essential contrast is between a state of affairs conceived as operating in consistent and lawful fashion and one where an indeterminism (of whatever sort) reigns. The former case may eventuate in the outlook of Western science as stated by Karl Pearson or in the attempt to control events by supernatural techniques or in "fatalistic" acceptance. The latter, however, may also have a "fatalistic" toning in a different sense: resignation to "taking things as they come" without rhyme or reason. The indeterminate emphasis may also take the form of extreme voluntarism (either human or divine), since nothing is held to be completely determined or determinable. The outcome in the case of both alternatives will depend upon how this emphasis is juxtaposed with other cultural emphases. Nevertheless, I believe this particular binary opposition to be of absolutely crucial significance.

1b. Unitary-Pluralistic. Is the world, including human life, thought of as a single manifold or as segmented into two or more spheres in which different principles prevail? At first glance this contrast might appear to be a special case of the first. Certainly it would seem logically probable that the unitary emphasis would be likely to be found where the mechanistic emphasis dominates. But there are innumerable instances of "mechanistic" cultures exhibiting the familiar dualisms of "sacred and profane," "mind and body," not merely as categories in a larger whole but as altogether separate realms governed by distinct "laws" and with one construed as more permanent and superior to the other. Conversely, the classical Greeks who believed in ineluctable laws had a profoundly unitary conception of life.

1c. "Evil"-"Good." Cultures ordinarily attribute to inanimate nature, to supernatural beings, and to human nature properties that are positively or negatively toned. Nature is threatening or beneficent;

the supernaturals may or may not be effectively propitiated; human nature is basically good or evil. To be sure, the judgments often— or perhaps usually—come in somewhat mixed or qualified form, but I suspect that one polarity or the other usually stands out. Emphasis upon "good" does not mean in the least that the problem of evil is ignored. Thus the Zunis show considerable fear of the evil intentions of individuals and groups outside the intimate household; they likewise are concerned with disaster from events of nature. Yet the Zunis still conceive the cosmos as fundamentally a good place. All things are in the final analysis benevolent functioning parts of a universal, timeless order. The dead join a legion of beneficent beings who stand ready to help those living at Zuni. The Navaho, on the other hand, who exhibit no more fear of witches and natural events than do the Zuni, nevertheless conceive the order of the universe as "evil" in the sense that it is dominantly harsh and implacable. The dead are neither happy nor beneficent. Dominance of the "evil" aspect in men or gods or both commonly leads to "the tragic sense of life," but this may also result from a belief in man's being at the mercy of the caprices of impersonal nature. Whether cultures take what Florence Kluckhohn calls the subjugated-to-nature, the in-nature, or the over-nature position depends upon how the mechanistic-indeterminate, good-evil, and active-acceptant value emphases are combined. Other combinations lead to dominance of optimistic, pessimistic, or resigned attitudes as dominant.

Cluster 2: MAN AND MAN. These emphases tone the relationship of persons to their fellows and their notions of themselves and their own goals. They also affect the human relationship to nature in so far as exploitation of resources and dominance over or submission to nature are concerned.

2a. Individual-Group. Is the individual or some collectivity (family, clan, local group, clique, occupational group, or tribe or nation) given priority? is the individual a means to the ends of some collectivity or vice versa?

2b. Self-Other. This refers to the relative emphasis placed upon egoism and altruism. The "other" consists in other individuals rather than in various solidary collectivities. For example, loyalty and devotion—at some expense to the interests of the self— are enjoined toward wife, children, and other relatives as persons rather than as a family entity. Or the emphasis may be directed primarily toward friends or occupational or ritual associates or to a god or gods. In any case the needs of the self are placed as high or low in reference to the needs of others (*as individual personalities*).

2c. Autonomy-Dependence. This contrast is closely related to the foregoing but is not coextensive with either. It is similar to Riesman's "inner-directed"-"other-directed" polarity. A culture, like that of the Soviet elite, may give clear primacy to group goals and yet insist sharply on the autonomous responsibility of the individual. Traditional Russian culture, on the other hand, also favored group goals but encouraged the dependence of the individual upon the group. Dominant American culture at present makes a fetish of "individualism," though one can think of few complex cultures where individuals are in fact so sensitive to the pressures of the ephemeral standards of the peer group. "Dominant" Americans are typically "individualistic" but rarely autonomous. Similarly, cultures like Kwakiutl or Plains Indian which support flagrant egoism demand at the same time dependence upon the group. Modern French culture would fall in the self-autonomy category, but medieval Christian culture accentuated altruism and personal autonomy simultaneously. All human beings have experienced dependence as infants and children. This is one of the universal "cues" from which value selection and elaboration take off. Cultures vary in the extent to which this dependence in different forms is extended into adult life or taken as the basis for reaction-formations.

2d. *Active-Acceptant.* This opposition is intimately tied to the determinate-indeterminate and autonomy-dependence pairs but is, again, not coextensive. Autonomy may take the active form of self-assertion or the passive form of withdrawal. The Epicureans postulated the existence of gods but believed that they too were bound by universal laws with the working-out of which the gods themselves were powerless to interfere. The Epicurean therefore accepted his lot with serene pessimism. The Buddhist also conceives of an order of things lawfully determined but intervenes very actively if only in a somewhat mechanical—and often withdrawing—way. The dichotomy is thus not strictly that between activity and acceptancy. The Spanish-Americans of New Mexico, to give another example, are acceptant but active in a "being" sort of way. They take Florence Kluckhohn's "subjugated-to-nature" position yet nevertheless are far from completely "passive."

2e. *Discipline-Fulfilment.* Roughly, this is the "Apollonian-Dionysian" contrast. The issue is between safety and adventure, between control and expansion, between "adjustment" to the culture and internal harmony. Cultures stressing the "evil" in nature are likely to give emphasis to discipline, yet some of these cultures do emphasize either the self-realizing or the orgiastic dimensions.

2f. *"Physical"-"Mental."* Are sensual or sensuous activities and reactions given a higher place in the hierarchy than the intellectualized? This is approximately Sheldon's "cerebrotonic" category versus his "somatotonic" and "viscerotonic" combined. This pair, once more, cuts across other pairs. Thus "discipline" may be predominantly motor or otherwise "physical" or may, on the other hand, be mainly artistic and intellectual.

2g. *Tense-Relaxed.* Aspects of culture other than sounds exhibit these pervasive qualities which refer to the whole style of life and the general tone of all, or most, activities. One might anticipate that cultures with value-emphasis upon autonomy and discipline are more likely to be "tense," but this tendency, if it exists, is by no means an exceptionless uniformity (cf. Table 1). Nor does "relaxed" deny the presence of anxiety or even fairly frequent paranoid-like suspicion. The test is the degree to which tension of any kind is pervasive or is more than balanced by some sense of humor and calm easy-goingness. This opposition could be called "intense-bland."

2h. *Now-Then.* Cultures vary widely and importantly in their conceptions of time as an unbroken continuum or as segmented by a moving present or as homogeneous and instantaneous. But from the angle of values the most significant accent would appear to be that upon the here-and-now as opposed to either past or future. The case of emphasis upon this life as contrasted with the hereafter is merely a special case of the now-then opposition.

Cluster 3: BOTH NATURE AND MAN. There are certain value-emphases where existential and evaluative assumptions are clearly linked. They also apply both to the nature of the external world and specifically to that of man.

3a. *Quality-Quantity.* This contrast will reflect the degree of measurement or other standardization other than purely qualitative found in the culture. It will also be manifest in the extent to which the culture indicates that the natural world and human experience can be atomized. Conceptions of space and time will be largely influenced by the prevalence or absence of concepts of quantity beyond ordinal and cardinal numeration.

3b. *Unique-General.* According to Northrop, this is the basic opposition between oriental cultures and those of the West, between the "undifferentiated aesthetic continuum" and "the method of logical postulation." Cultures emphasizing the individual event in all of its uniqueness are not, however, likely to be quantitative. Experience is too much of a sequence of events that may not properly be dismembered. Abstractions are either avoided or treated with great suspicion. The concrete and the literal are what count. Cultures, on the other hand, that favor the general are more interested in similarities than in differences. One sensitive index of this contrast is the tendency toward stereotyping present in the culture. In sum: discreteness and particularity contrasted with abstraction and universalism.

Discussion. Let me repeat: this is a system of priorities, not a set of all-or-none categories. Each member of a pair will have some representation in every culture if only in variant value-emphasis held by individuals or subgroups in the larger society. In some idea and behavior systems the secondary emphasis will be more prominent than in others. While in far the greater number of cases, cultures take a pretty definite position one way or the other, there are instances where it would be plainly false to ascribe a definite "choice." Thus the Spanish-Americans regard the evil-good pair not so much as "mixed" as "uncertain." Potentialities for human afterlife and for a divine order in the universe are religiously defined as "good." Though this variety of Catholicism does not take a fully Augustinian position on the evil in human nature, elements of this view are also present. But the decisive fact is that as regards the outcome of any particular set of events Spanish-American culture does not stress either evil or good. It simply says, in effect, "We do not know." In such cases one may follow the practice of linguists and call this a "zero-feature."

There are two other binary oppositions that are at a different conceptual level from the foregoing which they cut across. It makes a difference whether or not the dominant value-emphases are conscious in the sense of being frequently and easily verbalized. The explicit emphases become subject to rational consideration and criticism and are probably therefore more labile. The implicit emphases are taken for granted, almost as unchangeable conditions imposed by nature. The whole or the explicit culture is analogous to what the linguists call "langue" as contrasted with "parole," to "cultural phenotype" versus "cultural genotype." All of the assumptions and categories that are unconsciously begged in the implicit culture make up the "cultural genotype." Most of the core value-emphases in most cultures are—at any rate for the majority of the culture-carriers —"genotypic" in nature.

It would also appear to make a difference whether or not the core value-emphases take on a positive or a negative character. It is an induction from ordinary experience that the proportion of specific prescriptions (the "do's" and "dont's" of every culture) may be weighted more or less heavily in one direction or the other. It seems probable that the value-emphases are "felt" primarily as avoidances or as seekings.

Let us now examine the profiles one gets if one compares the profiles for the five southwestern cultures studied by the Harvard Values Project. They seem to me to come out as follows:

Mormon: determinate, unitary, good, group, other, dependence, active, discipline, "physical," tense, then, quantity, general.

Homesteader: indeterminate, pluralistic, evil, individual, self, autonomy, active, fulfilment,* "physical," relaxed,* then, quantity, general.

Spanish-Americans: indeterminate, unitary, zero-feature, individual,** other, dependence, acceptant, fulfilment, "mental," relaxed, now, quality, unique.

Zuni: determinate, unitary, good, group, self, dependence, active, discipline, "mental," relaxed, now, quality unique.

Navaho: determinate, pluralistic, evil, individual, self, dependence, active, fulfilment, "physical," tense, now, quality unique.

Some of these assignments are admittedly arguable. The weight of the evidence, however, strikes me as reasonably clear in most instances. The average disagreement between my own original independent ratings and those of the "experts" is just over one category per culture.

TABLE I

	Intermediate (2 cases)	Pluralistic (2 cases)	Good (2 cases)	Group (2 cases)	Other (2 cases)	Dependence (4 cases)	Acceptant (1 case)	Fulfilment (3 cases)	Mental (2 cases)	Relaxed (3 cases)	Then (2 cases)	Quantity (2 cases)	General (2 cases)
Determinate (3 cases)	. . .	1	2	2	1	3	0	1	1	1	1	1	1
Unitary (3 cases)	2	. . .	2	2	2	3	1	1	2	2	1	1	1
Evil (2 cases)	1	2	. . .	0	0	1	0	2	0	1	1	1	1
Individual (3 cases	2	2	0	. . .	1	2	1	3	1	2	1	1	1
Self (3 cases)	1	2	1	1	. . .	2	0	1	1	2	1	1	1
Autonomy (1 case)	1	1	0	0	0	. . .	0	1	0	2	1	1	1
Active (4 cases)	1	2	2	2	1	3	***	2	1	2	2	2	2
Discipline (2 cases)	0	0	2	2	1	2	0	. . .	1	1	1	1	1
Physical (3 cases)	1	2	1	1	1	2	0	2	. . .	1	2	2	2
Tense (2 cases)	0	1	1	1	1	2	0	1	0	. . .	1	1	1
Now (3 cases)	1	1	1	1	1	3	1	2	2	2	. . .	0	0
Quality (3 cases)	1	1	1	1	1	3	1	2	2	2	0	. . .	0
Unique (3 cases)	1	1	1	1	1	3	1	2	2	2	0	0	. . .

*There is a strong variant here: tense-disciplined. These could be called, following the linguistic analogy, "allo-values."
**The dominance of individual-other is quite recent.

In some of these cases the cultures in question have changed radically during the past generation. In making my ratings, I tended to weight the older values as expressed, for example, in myths, while some of my colleagues laid greater stress upon present attitudes and behavior. I think also that the profiles make sense in terms of more general information. Each total profile is completely distinct, but Mormon and Homesteader appear as variants of Protestant American culture, while the Spanish-American, which is a fusion of CatholicEuropean and Indian, stands somewhere between the Protestant and the Indian groups. Of the two Indian cultures, Zuni emerges as closer to Spanish-American, which is, again, expectable on historical grounds.

Table 1 (which was prepared after all assignments were final) shows ranges and combinations. "Quality" and "unique" give identical distributions, which suggests that they really represent only a single value-emphasis.* "Now" also gives an identical distribution, but it appears more doubtful that this is yet another instance of a single category. "Physical" and "tense" are fairly similar. "Evil" and "autonomy" bring out distinctions very sharply, but this may reflect the fact that only two cases and one case respectively, are involved.

A central problem in value theory is: What combinations are likely— or possible? Definitive results on this point could make possible a kind of "scaling" or a statement of the really fundamental value-emphases from which others could be derived. Hence, in spite of the fact that in a number of instances only a single opposition is involved, I have analyzed into relative distributions. Taking the value-emphases on the left-hand column of Table 1 as P and the horizontal column as Q, I distinguish as "complementary" those cases where the ranges of P and Q are mutually exclusive, as "coincident" those where they are the same, as "incorporating" the instances where the range of P is wholly included within the range of Q but not conversely, and as "overlapping" the cases where a part of the range of P is a part but not all of the range of Q.

1. *Complementary*
a. All of the original pairs (by definition)
b. determinate-acceptant, evil-group (good-individual), evil-other, evil-acceptant, evil-mental, self-acceptant, autonomy-good, autonomy-group, autonomy-other, autonomy-acceptant, autonomy-mental, discipline-indeterminate, discipline-pluralistic, discipline-acceptant, physical-acceptant, tense-indeterminate,

*They might well be collapsed under unique-general as being the more inclusive category.

tense-acceptant, tense-mental, now-quantity (then-quality),
now-general (then-unique), quality-general (quantity-unique)

2. *Coincident*
evil-pluralistic, evil-fulfilment, individual-fulfilment, discipline-good,
discipline-group

3. *Incorporating*
determinate-dependent, unitary-dependent, evil-fulfilment,
autonomy-indeterminate, autonomy-pluralistic, autonomy-fulfilment
autonomy-relaxed, autonomy-then, autonomy-quantity,
autonomy-general, discipline-dependent, tense-dependent,
now-dependent, quality-dependent, unique-dependent

4. *Overlapping*
All remaining cases.

It is also instructive to examine the relative distributions of the
converse pairs of value-emphases. It is worth noting that less than
half of these converse pairs fall in the complementary, coincident, or
incorporating categories. We will exclude those which are overlapping
as this is a residual category and contains all remaining pairs.
Further, in terms of relative distribution, it can be said that (1)
where the pairs of value-emphases are incorporating, the converse
pairs are not complementary; or where the pairs of value-emphases
are complementary, the converse pairs are not incorporating;
(2) where the pairs of value-emphases are coincident, the converse
pairs are not complementary; or where the pairs of value-emphases
are complementary, the converse pairs are not coincident.

There are four instances in which the value-emphases and their
converse pairs are both in complementary distribution:

evil-group	(good-individual)
now-quantity	(then-quality)
now-general	(then-unique)
quality-general	(quantity-unique)

This tends to confirm the suggestion that "quality," "unique," and
"now" are probably intimately related to a single value-emphasis.

There is but one instance where a pair of emphases is coincident both
as stated above and in the converse. The associated emphases
"individual-fulfilment" and the converse "group-discipline" occur
here, whereas "discipline-good" is coincident and the converse,
"fulfilment-evil," is incorporating. These cases suggest a possible
relationship among "group, "discipline," and "good."

Finally, in the incorporating category there are five pairs which are also incorporating in the converse:

autonomy-relaxed	(dependent-tense)
autonomy-fulfilment	(dependent-discipline)
autonomy-then	(dependent-now)
autonomy-quantity	(dependent-quality)
autonomy-general	(dependent-unique)

This seems to indicate that the value-emphases of "autonomy" or "dependence" are being incorporated in the distribution of the other emphases. It is worth noting that "quality," "unique," and "now" appear in similar distributions.

Of the thirteen original complementary pairs defined above, the following do not occur in any of the converse contexts but rather in the overlapping category:

determinate-indeterminate
unitary-pluralistic
self-other
active-acceptant
physical-mental

Perhaps this indicates a complexity which requires further distinctions or different conceptualizations. It is quite possible that the above pairs are not as "genuine" as the eight others and hence require redefinition.

Nothing could be more obvious than that the foregoing represents, at best, a point of departure rather than a point of arrival. I would argue that schemas of this general order need to be worked out theoretically and tried out empirically if cross-cultural comparison of values is to become comprehensive, parsimonious, and fruitful. In some way we must attain conceptual equivalence across cultural boundaries if more than the scientific *description* of values is to become possible.

References

Albert, Ethel M.
1956. The classification of values: a method and illustration. *American Anthropologist*, 58:221–48.
Kluckhohn, C.
1951a. Values and value-orientations in the theory of action. pp. 388–343 in: *Toward a General Theory of Action* (T. Parsons and E. Shils, eds.), Cambridge, Mass.: Harvard University Press.

1951b. A comparative study of values in five cultures. pp. vii-ix in: *Navaho Veterans, a study of Changing Values* by E. Z. Vogt. Papers of the Peabody Museum of Harvard University, vol. XLI, No. 1.
1956. Toward a comparison of value-emphases in different cultures. pp. 116–32 in: *The State of the Social Sciences* (L. White, ed.) Chicago: University of Chicago Press.
1958. The Scientific study of values and contemporary civilization. *Proceedings of the American Philosophical Society.* Vol. 102, No. 5, pp. 469–477.
Kluckhohn, F. and F. Strodtbeck.
1959. *Variations in Value Orientations.* Evanston, Illinois: Row, Peterson and Co.

SCIENCE, PURE AND APPLIED

by V. B. Wigglesworth, Quick Professor of Biology,
University of Cambridge

I t is a great honour, and a great responsibility, to be invited to give
one of the Installation Lectures on this auspicious occasion.
I am ill qualified for this task; but at least I may justly claim that
the subject on which I have chosen to speak is one that is of the
greatest importance to every university in every part of the world.

In England, at least, we sometimes forget that our universities
owe their origin and their development in great part to the demands
of practical affairs.

They arose in the Middle Ages, mainly to provide better education
for the hosts of 'clerks' or subordinate clergy who undertook all the
tasks in mediaeval society for which some degree of learning was
necessary.

With the great expansion of trade and affairs in England in Tudor
times there was a corresponding expansion of the Universities of
Oxford and Cambridge with an increased emphasis on medicine
and law.

At that time and later the universities were tolerably active and
effective; but after the violent disturbances of the Civil War and
Restoration there followed a long period of stagnation and privilege
extending throughout most of the eighteenth century.

Then came the Industrial Revolution. This was based on the
achievements of practical men, drawing upon the experience of
craftsmen; and England quickly climbed to a position of ascendancy
which for a time seemed unassailable. But there were far-seeing
people who soon perceived that such a position could not be
sustained unless techniques and procedures were continually improved,
and that the source of such improvement was to be found in the
natural sciences.

The turning point was the Great Exhibition of 1851. Although British
products were still outstanding, the progress that had been made by
our competitors, basing their techniques on scientific study and
research, was alarming. This was the immediate stimulus which led,

during the second half of the century, to the establishment of technological institutes of many kinds and to the foundation and expansion of a series of new universities. The depressed state of farming in this same period led to a corresponding improvement in agricultural education and in the development of the sciences basic to agriculture.

In our own time two World Wars have underlined the dependence of our present society upon science. And the demand for new sources of energy has led to a renewed expansion in teaching and research in science and technology, which is now in full swing.

But those of us who work in universities soon forget these origins. We forget, for example, that the standard course of zoology, as taught in most universities for the best part of a century, was the creation of Thomas Henry Huxley who was appointed to teach zoology in the Royal School of Mines in South Kensington; and that Huxley owed his appointment to the very practical need for mining prospectors, who could find their way among the strata of the earth by means of the fossils which these contain.

In this lecture I propose to consider the relation between pure and applied science. But first I must say a few words on the methods of science.

New knowledge in science comes in many different ways, but in the deliberate search for knowledge it is customary to recognize two quite distinct procedures. There is first that formulated by Francis Bacon and called by him the 'Novum Organum'. It consists in the accumulation of facts. These, it is anticipated, will eventually all fall into place; and without the exercise of any more thought than that required by a committee, a complete understanding of nature will be achieved. This method still has its advocates and its practitioners but it has always proved singularly unproductive.

The second method is the experimental method. This has often been described, perhaps nowhere better than by Claude Bernard a century ago in his *Experimental Medicine*. It consists in the formulation of an hypothesis which the investigator then attempts to prove, that is, to demolish, by a series of experiments. If all attempts fail, the hypothesis is provisionally accepted as a theory or base for further hypotheses; and thus the provisional edifice of scientific knowledge is gradually built up.

The essential ingredient is the hypothesis. Where does this come from? It comes, of course, from the imagination which formulates ideas. Claude Bernard describes graphically how the investigator outside the laboratory should allow his imagination full rein; but when he enters the laboratory he should shed his imagination like his overcoat. We all recognize that the progress of science is constantly dependent on improved techniques. But technique alone is not enough. (One has only to contemplate the wasted effort that can be expended on new techniques just because they are new.) When we say that we lack a knowledge of techniques, as often as not we mean that we lack ideas.

Where then do the ideas come from that form the basis of these precious hypotheses? They come by thought. But thought is a difficult and painful process: most people would rather die than think; and that is why they are so ready to escape the necessity by adopting empiricism, or Baconianism, which sometimes appears in modern dress as the substitution of statistics for thought. But in scientific research there is no substitute for thought. That is not a truth which we readily admit. We are glad enough to extol the merits of teamwork, to demand heavier endowments for research, and to admire fine equipment, but we are reluctant to speak of the necessity for thought and the generation of ideas.

But where do thoughts come from? To conceive good thoughts you need a good brain, and a brain prepared by education and experience to associate ideas and derive new conclusions from diverse observations. Even the best brains, however, do not operate in a vacuum. They are subject, among other things, to the influence of fashion. In science they may be led by fashion to pursue particular lines of study until these have become more and more specialized and less and less productive of important results.

Take the examples of muscular contraction or nerve conduction, both fields of research which have engaged the attention of highly specialized schools of physiologists for many years. From time to time these schools have looked like becoming so specialized as to produce results which none but their own members could understand. But always the subject has been revivified by ideas from outside. At the present time, with techniques and ideas coming from physical chemistry, biochemistry, nuclear physics, X-ray crytallography, electron optics, these subjects are once more in a most exciting phase of eruption.

Now one of the most efficient correctives to the dangers of over-specialization is provided by the stimulus of contact with practice. The research worker in pure science who has reached the point where his ideas are going round and round in circles like a bee in a bell-jar, may have a new direction and stimulus given to his work by contact with some practical problem. One is tempted to borrow the jargon of the dialectical materialists and claim that the interaction of the opposites of theory and practice, of pure and applied science, is one of the most potent dialectics in the advancement of knowledge.

The zoologist studying the natural history or autecology of an animal is generally satisfied with a comparatively superficial knowledge of it. After all, there are so many animals in the world to know about. But when the applied biologist is confronted with some animal in competition with man, a mosquito carrying yellow fever or malaria, a migratory locust, an aphid bringing virus diseases to the potato crop, a sawfly destroying the wheat crops of Alberta, he requires a depth of knowledge of quite a different order. It is in these fields that the principles of ecology are being hammered out. It is a question of personal preference whether we regard this as an example of the pure science of ecology coming to the rescue of the applied biologist or as an example of the applied biologist showing how ecology should be studied.

We see the same state of affairs in taxonomy. Taxonomy provides the essential basis of any work to do with living creatures; and that, of course, is the real justification for the existence of our museum staffs. But museum workers were slow to appreciate the full implications of Darwinism. Although the principle of evolution was soon accepted, the museum worker, almost of necessity and by the very nature of his work, has clung to the idea of the fixity of species. During the last fifty years the development of genetics and ecology has been changing that, and today we hear much of the "new systematics." But what is not always appreciated is the contribution of the applied biologist to this change in outlook. The museum worker has long recognized geographical races; but it has been the applied biologist, looking at his animals in nature, at all stages in their development, far more intimately than the museum worker could possibly do, who has realized that a single species may present a variety of "biological races" differentiated by their ways of life. Although it is requiring the painstaking work of the geneticist to analyse the nature of biological races and their relation to species formation, I do not think it would be an exaggeration to say that the discovery of these races was due to the applied biologist.

I have spoken of the need for thought. But one of the dangers by which science is beset is too much thought: an undue faith in the capacity of reason. For hundreds of years the great physicians of Europe based their medical practice upon systems of medicine which had been arrived at by a process of pure thought. And scarcely a vestige of those systems has remained: the purely rational process has indeed proved extraordinarily unproductive.

On the other hand, the scientific method has proved so amazingly successful during the past century or two that in these days reliance on pure reason is at a discount. Yet the risk of science, or parts of science, becoming enmeshed in some fabric of logic is by no means negligible. If one were to search the annals of current science I do not doubt that one would find small islands of scholasticism where existing theories are considered self-sufficient and the mind is satisfied with formal explanations in terms of these accepted theories. But the cold rude breath of experimental science blows everywhere and these sheltered corners do not remain undisturbed for long.

In the universities today there is a revival of interest in the philosophy of science, the study of logic and so-called "scientific method." There can be no doubt that these matters provide an admirable exercise for the mind—they will be harmful only if students come to believe that scientific knowledge is in fact built up and advanced by any such logical procedure.

In the past, in the absence of that organized body of fact and theory that we call science, no discovery had permanence unless it was incorporated into the traditional procedures of some practical art. And since it is very difficult to be sure whether a given change in the practice of an art represents progress or decay, the practitioners of such arts have always been extremely conservative. Indeed such a system of knowledge could remain stable only so long as it was intensely conservative.

Science has changed all that. A body of classified knowledge is being built up, held together and summarized by laws and theories which make possible an almost infinite number of predictions from a minimum of brief generalizations. We professional scientists know that all these generalizations are only provisional. They represent "summaries of current opinion," some of which may endure for a thousand years or more, like the Ptolemaic conception of the universe; others may last a century or two like the system of Copernicus, Galileo and Newton; while yet others, which we ordinary folk formulate, are destined to be current for no more than a few years at the most.

But the general public does not appreciate the provisional nature of scientific knowledge. It is no wonder that the practitioners of crafts of every kind have come to rely more and more on science and have developed a flattering faith in the opinions of the scientist. On the whole I believe that faith is well founded; but there have been many examples, even in the recent history of science, of scientists discrediting most valuable discoveries and beliefs because the knowledge and methods available to the science of the day have been inadequate.

There had long been a belief that fleas were connected with human plague; but when plague first appeared in India in 1896 and a strong scientific commission was appointed to investigate the matter they wrote in their report that "the theory that the plague is carried to man by some biting insect is scarcely worthy of statement." The transmission of plague by the rat flea was conclusively demonstrated a few years later. When my father was a medical student he was taught that one Steinhaeuser had claimed that rickets could be cured by the administration of cod-liver oil, but that, in fact, chemists had shown that cod-liver oil contained only the same sorts of fatty acids as olive oil, and since olive oil was much pleasanter to take it was just as well to prescribe that!

In medical practice the fungus-infected rye grains known as ergot have long been used to induce prolonged contraction of the uterus and so control post-partum haemorrhage. At one time this action was attributed to certain alkaloids present in the drug. But when I was a medical student I was taught that none of the characteristic alkaloids of ergot had this effect, and that any prolonged action of this kind upon smooth muscle which might be claimed by the doctors was simply due to the putrefactive bases, notably tyramine, which developed in the decomposing fungus. However, practising doctors, influenced I am afraid by an obstinate empiricism, continued to use extract of ergot for the treatment of post-partum haemorrhage, and this preparation continued to appear in the British Pharmacopoeia. Indeed, it was not until 1935 that Chassor Moir and Dudley reported that the watery extract of ergot did in fact contain an alkaloid "ergometrine," which had been overlooked by earlier workers, and that this alkaloid had just the properties for which the obstetricians had been using the drug for a century or more.

All this is not intended to depreciate the contribution of science to the practical arts but to illustrate the nature of that contribution. So very often it is not to *discover* some phenomenon of practical use, but ultimately (and sometimes long after that use has been adopted on purely empirical grounds) to provide a rational explanation for it. I submit that such rationalization is of the highest importance, for the two reasons I have already stated. First, because it gives stability and permanence to knowledge. Secondly, because there is a limit to the amount of empirical information which the mind can retain; when that knowledge has been given a rational basis it will appear as the necessary consequence of natural laws, and a few general laws may be sufficient to predict an infinite number of special properties. One has only to think of the predictions that are possible in organic chemistry with the aid of a comparatively limited number of general principles.

When the scientific method is brought to bear upon the practical arts it is *not* usually by the procedure of the hypothesis, the experiment, and the theory, but by the empirical method of direct experimentation. It must warm the heart of the applied scientist to quote John Hunter's famous advice to Jenner: "Don't think; try the experiment!" For to try experiments without too much thought is often the quickest way of arriving at a practical objective. When the limits attainable by such experimentation have been reached, scientific study of the problem may lead to a new outlook and provide the starting-point for a new empirical attack.

For man is an empirical animal. Each new advance in scientific discovery provides him with new weapons for his irrational procedure. His empiricism often leads to surprising observations which could never have been made if every step in the procedure had been rational. That, of course, is why bad experimenters can sometimes get results where good experimenters fail. Claude Bernard missed the presence of trypsin in the pancreatic juice because he was so skilful as a surgeon that he obtained juice uncontaminated by the contents of the duodenum and so the trypsinogen remained inactive. And how many new discoveries in organic chemistry have been made because the operator broke the thermometer and obtained syntheses catalyzed by mercury.

The production of a new material or a new process is soon followed by its trial for all kinds of purposes, a series of "experiments" the results of which may provide the basis for subsequent systematic investigation and rationalization by scientific research. We are impatient, and such random experiments are often the quickest way of getting results. A large part of scientific research consists in proving what we have already learned by such methods; scientific research is a slow way of gathering information, but information so obtained is more likely to survive.

In 1939 Paul Müller and his colleagues in Switzerland discovered the insecticidal properties of the chemical now known as D.D.T. In 1944, Läuger, Martin and Müller wrote up a fascinating account of the steps which led to the discovery. I do not pretend to know whether these were the logical steps which were actually followed or whether (as in the writings of most of us) the logic was inserted afterwards to give coherence to the story. What is quite certain is that few would now accept the toxicological basis of their argument, which turns on the hypothetical association of particular chemical groupings with particular types of toxicity. In the parallel case of the discovery of the gamma isomer of benzene hexachloride in England and France, there has never been any suggestion that this was a product of the human reason; it was discovered by the wholly empirical procedure

of testing as potential insecticides any chemical that chanced to
come to hand.

What immediately caught the eye was that both these chemicals
were heavily chlorinated aromatic compounds. The significance of
this has not yet been adequately explained, but it led chemists all
over the world to set about chlorinating every ring compound they
could think of; with the result that we now have upon the market a
further series of potent synthetic insecticides. Some day scientific
research will have to provide an understanding of these triumphs
of empiricism.

We have had an instructive example of the relation between
scientific research and applied biology in the problem of the fruit tree
Red Spider Mite, which has been engaging the attention of orchardists
increasingly in recent years. Ten years ago it was agreed as between
the Agricultural Research Council, a group of insecticide
manufacturers and the growers to undertake a joint attack upon
this problem. The investigation was planned upon a broad front.
Direct trials of insecticides were made against the mite and its eggs;
the life cycle and habits of the mite were studied in the field; its
relation in competition with the rest of the fauna of the orchards
was studied. In the laboratory, the behaviour of the mite, and the
nature and determination of the arrested development or diapause
in the overwintering egg were studied in great detail; and finally the
complex nature of the egg shell and its relation to the entry of
insecticides were partially unravelled.

As the result of ten years study we have now for the first time a real
understanding of the life of this mite. No one working on this
problem in the future can fail to benefit from all this knowledge
(incomplete though it is) which enables one to think intelligently
about this pest in a way which was quite impossible in the past,
and to utilize to some extent the natural fauna of the orchard as a
contributory factor in control. From the practical standpoint the
investigation was wholly successful, for new methods of control have
been introduced into the orchards which appear to have solved
the problem. But the interesting point is this: control is being effected
primarily by the use of summer ovicides. The production of these
ovicides was based, of course, upon a century of organic chemistry;
but from the standpoint of biology their discovery was wholly
empirical; it owed nothing to the scientific investigations of the
remainder of the team, and their mode of action is unknown!

That is not an experience which should in any way discourage the
student of the ecology or physiology of insects. Some years ago I
had the privilege of attending a luncheon in Winnipeg at which I

was asked to speak about the "contribution of insect physiology to medical entomology." The burden of my address was that it made no contribution; that is, no *direct* contribution, and it is not its function that it should.

I think that is a matter about which we should be clear. We often hear the young man sigh deeply and say: "It must have been wonderful when you were starting research and all the field was wide open. Nowadays it is different—everything easy has been done." And yet we all know that you have only to take up the most familiar matter in pure or applied science and almost at once you find that almost nothing is known about it. Indeed, most of us thank God for our ignorance, and happily contrast our lot with that of the classical scholar who has long since worked out his mine and is now reduced to picking over the slag heaps in the hope that he may have missed a little of the ore.

The prime contribution of pure science is to make good this deficiency in knowledge. Very rarely can the applied biologist or the applied scientist in general put his finger on some discovery in pure science and say that it was this which solved his problem— but in thinking about any practical problem he is continually making use of the whole range of scientific knowledge that exists about all its component parts.

When one reads the discourteous remarks that are made in certain quarters about "reactionary mendelismus—morganismus" one might imagine that the professional breeders of plants and animals in Western Europe and the Americas were all geneticists. Nothing, of course, could be farther from the truth. Most of the complex systems with which the breeder is concerned are still beyond the grasp of the geneticist—or he is only just beginning to extend his science to include them. In very many instances, breeding is still an empirical art which relies on gifts of intuition and experience. Even the production of hybrid corn, which is often claimed as one of the practical triumphs of genetics, although based upon a most penetrating genetical analysis, could be fairly described as the result of an informed empiricism operating on a grand scale. The production of the mule, that other classic example of hybrid vigour, certainly owed nothing to Mendel.

No! The role of the geneticist has consisted largely in explaining what the animal or plant breeder has already done. By so doing he gives stability to knowledge, provides starting-points for further empirical steps, and, what is perhaps of equal importance, he provides the background or climate of thought.

I made my approach to the physiology of reproduction and inheritance by the historical method. My early researches were conducted in an ancient volume of Buffon's *Natural History* which I discovered in the lumber room; and I waded through the controversy on whether the female contributes anything to the embryo at conception. Then a year or two later I came across a translation of Haeckel and learned all about the amazing story of the ovum and the spermatozoon. Finally, this must have been about forty-five years ago, I noticed a slim little volume in the school library entitled *"Mendelism"*; and being curious to know what on earth mendelism might be I took it down and read all about the particulate inheritance of characters. I am afraid that my knowledge of the subject has not greatly advanced since those days. But what an astonishing range of ideas one is left with: the independent inheritance of characters; recessive characters uninfluenced in heredity by the dominant characters in the zygote; the equal contribution of the sexes; the reappearance of characters in later generations by recombination, and so on and so forth. My point is that even genetics at its simplest provides an indispensable background for thought for the breeder of plants and animals, which he will inevitably have in mind even when he uses such more or less empirical procedures as progeny selection or hybridization.

This background of scientific knowledge may find its application in quite remote fields of practice. Think, for example, of the preparation of food. During the present century there have been remarkable advances in physical chemistry and colloid science; and it has come to be realized that many of the finer products of cooking owe their special qualities to the physico-chemical properties of the traditional ingredients. The ingredients in question are often the expensive ones like egg albumen and cream. But armed with this knowledge it has not proved an insuperable task for the colloid chemist to produce cheap substitutes from gelatin, seaweed, soya beans and the like which have approximately the same properties for the specific purposes required. This has been a most profitable achievement. As a result, millions of our people have never tasted those exquisite delicacies: meringues, ice creams, sponge cakes, cream buns or lemon curd. We hear much about the moral responsibility of the atomic physicist. Some might feel that the colloid chemist must have a heavy conscience when he views this field of applied biology. (Although, of course, he can tell himself that these young people have never known what real food was and therefore cannot feel its loss.)

In reading a recent report from the Pest Infestation Laboratory I was struck by that section which describes how the kaffirs in South Africa complained that since the introduction of hammer mills for grinding maize (in place of the ancient pestle and mortar or grinding between stones) the flour did not taste the same and it upset the stomach. Examination in the laboratory revealed the presence of numerous rodent hairs and some 22,000 insect fragments per 25 gm. of the meal. One is inevitably reminded of the homogenizer, another contribution of technology to the preparation of food which is equally liable to abuse. I recently enjoyed some soup in a well-known London hotel which (having kept hens during the war) I had no difficulty in recognizing as homogenized vegetable peelings.

This brief sketch of the recent history of cooking almost inevitably leads to a consideration of the allied science of immunology. The familiar history of immunization as a practical craft can be traced from the practise of inoculation against smallpox in Constantinople and elsewhere in the East and its introduction into England by Lady Mary Wortley Montague. This was followed by the equally empirical procedure of vaccination developed by Jenner from the traditional observations of peasants. The efficiency of vaccination was proved by Jenner by careful experiment. It was followed in the succeeding century, during the golden age of bacteriology, in the hands of Pasteur and his successors, by a whole series of immunizing procedures against various pathogenic organisms. These practices, an elaborate form of cookery, are still extremely valuable in medicine, but we are still almost completely ignorant of the nature of the immunizing process—and indeed of the whole mechanism of protection by the body against infective organisms. The systematic study of these matters is the science of immunology, the key to which is likewise held by biochemistry and colloid science. The utilization of artificial immunization in practice is scientific only in the sense that what are essentially empirical procedures have been reduced to some degree of order by careful experiment.

There is, indeed, no hard and fast line between what I am calling empiricism or direct experiment and what I am calling scientific research. Both are supported by the same implicit faith in the constancy of natural laws—a faith so absolute that few other religious faiths can equal it. The spread of this faith among people of every kind is perhaps the greatest of all the contributions of pure science to every day life. It is certainly one of the major contributions of science to medicine or to farming.

I am far from supposing that such convictions are universal; there is still a widespread belief in magic—which often masquerades as a belief in science. If we were to take a free vote among the English people I think there is little doubt that we should find a majority in favour of the spontaneous generation of complex organisms, a phenomenon which most biologists would class with the miraculous. Nor am I suggesting for a moment that the doctor should always be made to "think scientifically"; this is, "to adopt the mental process necessary for the satisfactory pursuit of experimental science: to demand severe standards of evidence and proof, to draw no conclusion that is not strictly justified by the evidence, to leave in suspense any decision for which the materials are not quite complete." The last thing the doctor can afford to do is to exercise scientific suspense of judgement. To advise him to think scientifically would risk paralyzing his judgement rather than activating it. No! the practice of medicine, like the practice of government, is a practical art which demands not the limited instrument of the scientific method but a soundly cultivated judgement. And one element in the cultivation of that judgement I hold to be a sympathetic familiarity with the outlook and achievements of science, pure and applied. That is all the more necessary today, when, as part of his improved technique, the charlatan adopts the language of science (that itself is indeed a highly lucrative form of applied science) and it is no easy matter to distinguish the genuine from the spurious.

Thus far we have been thinking mostly of the past. What of the present and the future? How are we to ensure that the pure sciences, the roots of the tree which provides such valuable fruit for all men, are helped and encouraged to grow unimpeded?

It is the universities which cherish the tradition of free enquiry in science—uninfluenced by any considerations of possible usefulness. We must have a wide margin of enthusiasts in the universities whose enquiries are *totally* unrestricted. Not only is that desirable in the interests of learning, it is absolutely necessary in order to safeguard the applied science of tomorrow.

For it is notoriously difficult to foresee just which discoveries in pure science will prove to be of practical value. When writing the first edition of his *Grammar of Science* in 1892, Karl Pearson chose as an example of a discovery which had no apparent practical value, the recently described Hertzian waves, the waves of radio. And who could possibly have foreseen where the infant organic chemistry of 120 years ago was going to lead—for at that time it had no conceivable connection with industry? Who can foresee today where theoretical chemistry is going to lead? It is possible that this may provide the real key to the biology, medicine and industry of the future!

But the fact remains that as all the costs of running a university increase, a relatively greater proportion of the total funds available is deflected away from the costs of research. As a result, the head of a university science department who wishes to develop the research work of his team must seek outside aid.

This almost always involves seeking extra financial support from one or other of the Research Councils. In Great Britain we have three such Councils concerned respectively with Medicine, Agriculture and Industry. Thus they all have practical objectives.

The Research Councils have always interpreted the needs of applied science in a most liberal and enlightened way. The Department of Scientific and Industrial Research, for example, makes grants for any research projects which are judged to be of exceptional "timeliness and promise." The difficulty is that the most original ideas are at the outset both unpromising and untimely. Only research which is totally unfettered can advance into the most unpromising fields. And, in any case, a research project with some obvious practical importance very rightly makes the strongest appeal.

The threat to fundamental science is therefore real, and in the future it could become serious. The problem is universal. Writing of conditions in the United States, Professor Paul Weiss has pointed out that the system of allocating grants for a specific purpose is admirably suited for development work or for organizing trials of some existing theory; it is not suited for encouraging the most original research. He suggests that all organizations which contribute financially to the development of medicine, for example, should assign a fixed fraction of their budgets, perhaps no more than 10 per cent, to a common pool for the promotion of the biological sciences as such— this pool to be used as a mobile reserve, without restrictions, for the support and encouragement of men with ideas.

In Sweden the problem has been met by the establishment of a fourth council—a council for pure science. In Norway a steeply rising tax is levied on the profits of the "Football Pools" (the betting on English football!). In Denmark a great part of the profits of the Carlsberg brewery is earmarked by the Carlsberg Foundation for general scientific research.

We sometimes hear complaints that the universities are not interested in the needs of the applied sciences. I hope I have said enough to make clear my conviction that some contact with the requirements of industry (including, of course, agriculture and medicine in that term) can be extremely stimulating for the research worker in pure science. But it would be most dangerous to go further than that. Knowledge is a delicate plant—and to keep pulling plants up to see how the roots are getting on is not the best way to encourage their growth.

Pure science provides the tools that can be applied for man's benefit. When and where these new tools are going to be produced is utterly unpredictable and is not amenable to planning. Perhaps we are too inclined to think of these tools as things like wireless waves, or antibiotics, or vitamins, or new insecticides, or hormone weed killers. But these are only valuable side products of pure science. The primary objective of science is to provide the theories which are the tools of thought. To equip the mind with *these* tools is, I submit, the real contribution of pure science to practical affairs.

DESIGNED BY HAROLD KURSCHENSKA

FOR THE DEPARTMENT OF INFORMATION AND PUBLICITY

PUBLISHED BY THE UNIVERSITY OF TORONTO PRESS